T0090303

Radka MacGregor Pelikánová
Jan Hejda
Andrea Schelleová
Karel Schelle
Jaromír Tauchen

An Overview of the Czech Commercial Law

Authors:
Radka MacGregor Pelikánová – Chapter 3
Jan Hejda – Chapter 2
Andrea Schelleová – Chapter 4
Karel Schelle – Chapter 1, 4
Jaromír Tauchen – Chapter 1

Order this book online at www.trafford.com
or email orders@trafford.com

Most Trafford titles are also available at major online book retailers.

Printed in the United States of America.

ISBN: 978-1-4269-4618-9 (sc)
ISBN: 978-1-4269-4619-6 (e)

*Our mission is to efficiently provide the world's finest, most comprehensive book publishing
service, enabling every author to experience success. To find out how to publish your book,
your way, and have it available worldwide, visit us online at www.trafford.com*

Trafford rev. 10/08/2010

 www.trafford.com

North America & international
toll-free: 1 888 232 4444 (USA & Canada)
phone: 250 383 6864 ♦ fax: 812 355 4082

CONTENTS

1. INTRODUCTION

1.1 ORIGINS OF COMMERCIAL LAW IN THE TERRITORY OF THE CZECH REPUBLIC

Commercial law was only restored in the Czech legal system after 1989, however it could pick up the threads of rich traditions going back to the ancient times. This is why we have to point out the basic landmarks of the evolution of commercial law in the territory of the Czech Republic.

Commercial law arises and starts do develop hand in hand with the emergence of the first towns which represented centres of craft and commerce. The foundations for the emergence of medieval towns are seen in town privileges granted to the town by its founders by the time of its foundation. Such privileges consisted in the establishment of internal organization and administration system of the town, delimitation of the citizens' obligations, law which they were to abide by and authorization to administer justice and carry out administration. This can therefore be referred to as a case of town autonomy, a right to issue its own regulations and town self-government, i.e. right to govern and administer its own issues by its own authorities.

With time, as towns were being founded, the need to codify town laws arose. The foundations for this were laid in town privileges as well as in the practice of own courts which is documented in the Brno Book of John the scribe (Kniha písaře Jana). This book was later reworked and extended by Brikcí of Licko and titled as the Town laws. The most significant work of codification was unquestionably the Code of Koldín called the Town Laws of the Czech Kingdom which was issued in 1579 and 1580 and it became binding for the then judicial practice. This code of law was in effect also in the 18th century and it was only gradually replaced and annulled by the legal codes of feudal absolutism. The last significant part of the code regarding property law was abolished as late as in 1811 by the General Civil Code.

The first European codification purely regarding commercial law was the "Code de commerce" created by Napoleon in 1807 which was meant to be the basis of the "droit commun de l'Europe". However, the Bohemian lands had to wait for a similar codification for several decades to come. While the codification efforts in the area of civil and family law culminated by the publication of General Civil Code in 1811, in the area of commercial law there was no such codification by then. Nevertheless, the gateway to modern commercial law was opened.

However, the work on the unification of commercial law was in progress since as early as 1809 when codification work was started. These effort, however, did not bring the expected results. Under these circumstances, at the federal convention of German states on April 17th of 1856, a resolution was adopted on establishing a special committee which was assigned the task of preparing a draft of a new legal code. In 1861, the work of this committee resulted in a draft of Commercial Code which was presented at the federal convention and it was recommended by a resolution of this convention to be approved and adopted by the states. Austria adopted the draft in the form of a bill of December 17th 1862 effective as of July 1st 1863 and this law was promulgated under number 1/1863. However, Austria did not adopt the entire code since it refused to accept the fifth book regarding the maritime law and so the existing legal provisions remained in effect. The adopted code was designated as the General Commercial Code (ADGHB). The indisputable advantage of the new code can be seen in the fact that it annulled all existing laws and regulations which were related to the subject of commercial code unless otherwise provided.

1.2 DEVELOPMENT OF COMMERCIAL LAW SINCE THE ESTABLISHMENT OF THE CZECHOSLOVAK REPUBLIC TILL THE GERMAN OCCUPATION

The independent Czechoslovak Republic was established on October 28th 1918 when its official independence was proclaimed by the National Committee. On the same day, at the plenary session of the National Committee, a new norm was adopted creating the mainstay of the entire legal system of the newly formed state. It was the "reception norm" as it was called, published in the statute book under number 11. According to this law, all existing provincial and imperial laws and regulations remained in effect and all authorities whether independent, national or municipal ones were subordinated to the National Committee.

The Reception law thus implied the adoption of the Austrian and Hungarian legal system. While in the Czech lands the General Civil Code remained the main source of law as it was subsequently amended, in Slovakia and the Carpathian Ruthenia the foundations of commercial law lay in legal article XXXVII – the "Slovak commercial code" as it was called, as subsequently amended. The need of new unified codification showed to be essential because it was necessary for the development of the economy within the entire state to unify the existing norms and regulations by means of a new codification of commercial law.

After long-lasting procrastination based on the pretext that it was necessary to codify the civil law first, the Ministry of Justice finally set up a committee for the unification of commercial law in 1929. In 1937 its activity resulted in the creation of a draft structure of the Commercial Code which was published in print but the draft was virtually just a torso of the desirable commercial law provisions. If the code had been adopted in its draft form it would have been less comprehensive than the analogous Hungarian code and even less comprehensive than the then effective fragmental Austrian Commercial Code.

The attempt to create a new codification of commercial law could not be carried through because the entire process was interrupted by the German occupation. The only attempt to bring closer together both systems existing within the territory of the republic can be seen in the law No. 271/1927 which extended the effect of the imperial law No. 58 of 1906 regarding limited liability companies for Slovakia and the Carpathian Ruthenia.

Throughout the entire duration of the interwar Czechoslovak Republic, the basis of commercial law lay in the General Civil Code adopted by the Reception law. The system of commercial law, however, was supplemented by law No. 111/1927 regarding unfair competition. Unfair competition was defined for one thing by a general clause and for another by individual states of facts defining the most frequent types of conduct in breach of fair competition. Finally, legal provisions regarding bills of exchange were codified by law No. 1/1928.

In the thirties, similarly to other countries, also in the Czechoslovak Republic there was a growing domination of the market by monopoly corporations and there was an increasing departure from economic liberalism. The most important regulation regarding this area was law No. 41/1933 on cartels and private monopolies. This law defined cartel agreements as agreements between independent entrepreneurs by which the parties are bound to limit or eliminate mutual economic competition by adjustments to production, sales, terms and conditions, prices or in case of transportation, credit or insurance companies, also to rates, if such agreements are aimed at dominating the market in the most efficiently. Cartel agreements always had to be made in writing. The cartel law also established the institute of cartel register together with a collection of documents which was kept by the statistical office.

1.3 DEVELOPMENT OF COMMERCIAL LAW DURING THE PROTECTORATE OF BOHEMIA AND MORAVIA

There was a double legal system during the Protectorate of Bohemia and Moravia – the protectorate law and the German Reichs law. Its application was dependent on the citizenship of the subjects of legal relations. Citizens of the Protectorate were subject to the law of Czechoslovak republic received after March 15th 1939 together with the newly adopted protectorate regulations which means primarily the "General Commercial Code". Citizens of the Third Reich were subject to the Commercial Code effective from 1897 (RGBl. I., S. 219).

During the war period, there were interferences in the provisions of commercial law by the state. The Minister of Justice had wide authorities and authorizations to take action especially in order to maintain public order or in relation to the wartime circumstances, limitations or exemptions from obligations laid down by commercial law regulations. That affected above all the obligation to publish the annual final accounts and the like. (Executive order No. 312/1942 regarding the exemption from obligation to abide by the commercial law regulations). The state also significantly regulated trading of securities which could not be sold outside the stock exchange at a price higher than that currently effective at the Prague stock exchange (Executive order No. 137/1941 regarding securities trading).

In connection with the implementation of forced labour under the Third Reich, various exemptions were introduced in 1944 for some areas of private law. This referred for example to the suspension of limitation periods or a ban on the transformation of joint-stock companies into limited liability companies (Regulation by the Minister of Justice No. 228/1944).

Similarly to the Reich, also under the Protectorate Jews were subject to racial persecution. Jews were not allowed to run and later even to own business enterprises as well as own securities. Such property and assets of the Protectorate citizens would often pass into the hands of German occupiers who thus tried to take control of the economy under the Protectorate.

1.4 EXTINCTION OF COMMERCIAL LAW AS A BRANCH OF LAW

After 1945 the legal system of the pre-war Czechoslovakia was preserved, but its basic principles and institutes were being dissipated, abolished or remained in effect only formally. Thus in Bohemia the Czech Commercial Code continued in effect for a short period as did the Slovak Commercial Code in Slovakia but the changes which took place in the organization of the post-war economy and especially the process of nationalization and introduction of planned economy brought about significant changes. The goal of the changes implemented during this period was to create a centralized economy based on the principle of economic planning and subjecting the economy to administration authorities.

After 1948, elimination of private enterprise and market economy took place. Basic changes in the development of legislation were brought about by the "legal two-year plan" as it was called (1949 - 1950). Some institutes of commercial law (such as procuration) were surviving within the "middle" Civil Code No. 141/1950 but in large part they were eliminated. The Civil Code abolished the Commercial Code without replacing it by another norm providing for commercial law. Thus, for the first time since the first modern codifications, a situation occurred where no specific provisions of commercial law were in place at all. Only some institutes were transferred into the Civil Code. Therefore it can be said that by creating the Civil Code, commercial law was abolished as a legal branch.

The planned economy, however, necessitated certain legal regulations. First of all, it was necessary to legally regulate relations between economic entities. Therefore in 1958, a law No. 69/1958 was enacted regarding economic relations between socialist organizations providing for a wide range or property relations between socialist organizations.

1.5 FORMATION OF ECONOMIC LAW

The requirement of codification of economic relations in a comprehensive form arose in 1960 in connection with the issuance of the Socialist constitution, as it was termed. Their legal regulation was incorporated into the economic code No. 109/1964 which provided for the relations arising during the management of national economy and when managing the economic activities of socialist organizations. Thus, a new branch of law was formed – the Economic law. This code together with the new Civil Code and the International Trade Code created a three-pronged code providing for property relations. The Commercial Code remained in effect until January 1st 1992 when, among others, a new commercial code was enacted and together with the amendment to the existing Civil Code and that is when the International Trade Code was abolished.

1.6 RESTORATION OF COMMERCIAL LAW AS A SEPARATE BRANCH OF LAW AFTER 1989

The political and economic changes following 1989 necessitated also fundamental changes in the area of legal system. The Economic Code, although it had been amended several times, became obsolete and absolutely unsuitable. Therefore it was necessary to return to the traditional commercial law.

That is why a new commercial code was being prepared and subsequently approved and published under No. 513/1991 which became effective on January 1st 1992. Within the transition to free market, all forms of ownership were put on an equal footing in terms of law, persons were granted the right of association for the purpose of carrying on business and a legal protective public framework was created in the form of a business register and trade law.

The year 2004 was significant in terms of the development of the Czech commercial law, because that is when the Czech Republic joined the EU on May 1st 2004. This step gave the law of EU absolute priority to the national law and the primary law together with the directly effective EU regulations and directives became directly applicable within the territory of the Czech Republic. In the spirit of these changes, the Czech Republic as EU member state observes the principles of European law and it is obliged to ensure applicability of these regulations and proper compliance of the national legislation with the requirements of European legislation.

1.7 CHARACTERISTICS AND STRUCTURE OF THE COMMERCIAL CODE AND COMMERCIAL LAW

The Commercial Code provides for the status of entrepreneurs, contractual relationships as well as some other relations related to business activities.

The Commercial Code consists of four parts:

1. Part one: General provisions (here, the basic terms such as the entrepreneur, business, enterprise, business capital, business conduct, procuration, trade secret etc. are defined. Further contained are the provisions regarding business activities of foreign persons in the Czech Republic, business register, business accounting and economic competition.)

2. Part two: Trading companies and cooperatives
3. Part three: Contractual relationships
4. Part four: Common provisions, transitional and final provisions

Other sources of law applied in the Czech commercial law are:

1. Civil law provisions (especially the Civil Code)
2. Business customs
3. Principles of commercial law

The basic principles of commercial law are:

1. Principle of autonomy of the will and freedom of contract
2. Principle of equality of the parties in contractual relationships
3. Principle of good will and protection of third persons
4. Principle of fair commercial intercourse
5. Principle of professionalism.

The commercial code constitutes a part of private law where the Civil Code plays the major role. The Commercial Code represents "lex specialis" in relation to the Civil Code, which me (put in simple terms) means that in cases where some issues are not provided for or only partially provided for by the Commercial Code, the Civil Code is applied. These issues will be discussed in more detail in the following chapters.

In other parts of this publication we will deal in more detail with the basic areas provided for by the Commercial Code and that is, trading companies and contractual relationships. Further we will briefly look into the issues of economic competition.

2. Commercial companies

2.1 Common reading

2.1.1 The term

Commercial companies represent legal entities incorporated to business, being registered by Companies Register and declared to be commercial companies by Commercial Code. The Code also contains majority of legal regulations related to commercial companies. The Commercial Code attends to commercial companies in its General Part, where concepts common to all commercial companies are explained, followed by its Special Part, which attends only to specifics of particular types of commercial companies. Except of the Commercial Code, a line of other regulations exists, containing special questions of particular commercial companies' forms that need to be provided by special regulations, different from general legal regulations of commercial companies. Czech legal system therefore counts specific legal entities, particularly European private company, European economic interest group, banks, investment companies and funds, joint-stock markets, savings banks, insurance companies, and pension funds.

Legal regulations of commercial companies are included in following legal regulations:

- Commercial Code (General Part and Special Part - Commercial companies),
- Special national legal regulations setting variations from Commercial Code regulations,
- European Community.
- Commercial companies within the meaning of the Commercial Code are following:
- General commercial partnership,

- Limited partnership,
- Limited liability company,
- Public company limited by shares,
- European private company,
- European economic interest group.

All abovementioned legal entities are declared to be commercial companies by the Commercial Code and are mandatorily registered by Companies Register. All types of commercial companies, barring limited liability companies and public companies limited by shares, must be incorporated to business. As all commercial companies are registered by Companies Register, they should be considered to be businesss. In accordance with the Commercial Code, everyone registered by Companies Register is considered to be an business, therefore should be foresaid applied even to limited liability companies and public companies limited by shares incorporated for different purpose than business. In case of not enterprising limited liability company or Public company limited by shares, it is a case of so called "business in form".

Commercial companies should be distinguished between personal and capital companies. General commercial partnership and limited partnership are traditionally referred to personal companies. Limited liability company and Public company limited by shares are traditionally referred to capital companies. Distinguishing criteria for personal and capital companies are especially following:

- Partners' personal concern in activities of the company,
- Partners' investment commitment,
- Partners' liability for company commitments.

General commercial partnership is from aforementioned considered to be so called "clear form" of personal commercial company. Partners of the partnership take active part in activities of the company and act on behalf of the partnership to third party. Partners do not have obligatory investments and they guarantee partnership liability with their total assets. This form of commercial company arose in past as a group of a small number of individuals, merchants or craftsmen, who ran their business together, their co-operative activity was necessary to meet their common target. A partner of a general commercial partnership mustn't be an unlimited partner guaranteeing another general commercial partnership, or a general partner of a limited partnership.

However a limited partnership is considered to be a personal commercial company, it shows characteristics of capital companies as well. This form of company developed historically as an intermediate stage between general commercial partnership, concentrating a small number of personally active individuals, and Public company limited by shares, concentrating considerable amount of property, which was administered by professional administration for common purposes. A limited partnership has two types of partners: general partners and limited partners. General partners do not have obligatory investments of the partnership, take active part in activities of the company and they guarantee partnership liability with their total assets. Limited partners are obligated to invest at least CZK 5000. They are not obligated to take an active part in activities of the company and are liable for the company's liabilities only sum amounting to their unpaid investment. It is evident from above-mentioned, that general partners' legal status is very similar to legal status of partners of general commercial partnership. On the other hand, limited partners' legal status, and some related legal relationships of the company, show significant similarity to limited liability company and its partners' status. For above-mentioned reasons, a limited partnership is in many respects close to capital commercial companies as it shows many of their characteristics. A general partner mustn't be a partner of a general commercial partnership or a general partner of another limited partnership.

A limited liability company is the newest in terms of development of traditional types of commercial companies. It arose not for need of practice, but as a result of legislators' decision and need of an intermediate stage between a general commercial partnership and a capital company, which should show features of capital commercial companies. Limited partners are obligated to invest at least CZK 20.000 and this investment should be fully paid within five years from company's incompany. Partners are liable for the company's liabilities only sum amounting to unpaid investments of all partners in total. Partners, as a governing body, may, but not have to, act on behalf of the company to third party.

Public company limited by shares arose historically for need of huge capital concentration, administered by a professional administration. The need appeared especially in relation to overseas discoveries and railway invention and building. Joint-stockholders of the company are not liable for company's liabilities, their obligatory investment is stated in accordance with rate of issue and they may, but not have to, as company authorities members take part in company administration and act on behalf of the company to third party.

European private company presents a commercial company that was formed to meet EU states effort towards unity legal regulations of this form of commercial company. As the original idea of unity of national legal regulations of Public company limited by shares proved impracticable, there was no other alternative but form a "multinational form of a commercial company – capital type", which enables cross-border businessship, especially in the area of EU. The legal form of commercial company is therefore regulated especially by the Commercial Code, Act. No 627/2004, About European private company; regulation of European Council No 2157/2001/ES, About European private company; and related EU directive No 200/86/ES, which amends the status of European private company with respect to employees engagement.

European economic interest group's formation is similar as well as the system. It is regulated especially by Act No 360/2004, About European economic interest group (EEIG), EC regulation (EEC) No 2137/85 from 1985/07/25 About European economic interest group (EEIG) incorporation.

2.1.2 INCORPORATION AND FORMATION

Czech commercial law strictly differentiates incorporation from formation of a company. From the view of transaction, the Commercial Code does not bind the possibility to on behalf of the company by the moment of formation, but admits to act on behalf of the company before its formation and regardless of the moment of company incorporation. It is possible therefore to look on three development stages in point of commercial company development: 1/ interlocutory commercial company, 2/ incorporated commercial company and 3/ originated commercial company.

It is possible to act on behalf of the company even before its formation and regardless of the moment of company incorporation, formation or the fact, whether the commercial company, on behalf of which it has been acted, will be incorporated or originated. It is possible to act on behalf of the "interlocutory commercial company" whenever before its formation. Neither circle of persons who may act on behalf of the interlocutory commercial company, nor the matters, they consider before company formation, are limited. It may be said, everyone may act on behalf of hitherto not incorporated or not originated company in whatever matters, whenever needed, before its formation. In such a case, the acting person negotiates a contract, but states his personal identification as well. From the point of the creditor's protection, in such a case of negotiator, it is necessary, regardless of incorporation or formation realized, to have his contracting party bound by the contract. The structure of contractual liability shows, that the negotiator is bound on the basis of acts made, i.e. the negotiator is liable, as well as obligee, unless the originated company, on behalf of which all has been negotiated, possibly assumes this legal proceedings. If the intended commercial company does not originate, or the originated company does not assume negotiation, it stays aloof from the contractual relationship, the person who acted stays an obligee or liable from the negotiation. In the event that it was acted on behalf of the commercial company before its incorporation or formation, acting persons are, from the point of incurred damage prevention, obligated to give notice about their actions to the governing authority. The governing authority will afterwards do listing of actions, which occurred before company formation, the list will be submitted to supreme company authority to decide which from the actions will be assumed and which will not by the commercial company. The decision must be made till three months from commercial company formation. If the supreme company authority decides to assume actions made, the company is bound by the actions made from the outset, on the basis of legal fiction. After actions made approval and their assumption, the governing authority notifies the contracting parties, having negotiated contracts before commercial company formation, of the fact. That means these contracting parties have their contracting partner in all circumstances.

A commercial company is incorporated at the moment of deed of incorporation signing, that is Memorandum of Association for General commercial partnership, Limited partnership and Limited liability company. In case of Public company limited by shares, Memorandum of Association and Articles of Association are deed of incorporations. As a Limited liability company and Public company limited by shares may be incorporated by a sole incorporator, in such a case a deed of incorporation is a deed of incorporation, which should meet the same requirements as a Memorandum of Association. The requirements of deed of incorporations are regulated by the Commercial Code for each particular commercial company. Deed of incorporations should be in a written form and partners' signatures should be attested. In a case of a limited liability company and a Public company limited by shares the deed of incorporation should have a form of notarial deed as well. A commercial company is therefore incorporated at the moment of concluding, or more precisely at the moment of signing the deed of incorporation. If the form of notarial deed to conclude a commercial company is required, the same form is required for a decision on its amendments or cancellation. A commercial company may be concluded for a definite period of time or for an indefinite period of time. Partners of the company are entitled to limit the period of time of company's existence in the deed of incorporation.

However, a commercial company does not acquire legal personality at the moment of concluding. A commercial company acquires legal personality at the moment of registration into the Companies Register. A commercial company may be registered solely on basis of application, but an authorized person only may apply, stated for each particular form of commercial company by the Commercial Code. In a case of personal commercial companies, all partners are authorized persons. In a case of stock corporations, all members of governing body are authorized. To register a commercial company, it is necessary to apply at an appropriate court, keeping the Companies Register, present appendices specified by the Commercial Code, and meet other requirements for commercial company incorporation. The basic appendices are particularly a deed of incorporation, paid-up contingent investment connameation or its necessary part, registered office location connameation, affidavit and other documents of company bodies' members, proving their satisfying the requirements of their office, and other. At the moment of commercial company is incorporated, the Companies Register publishes basic identification data of the commercial company and lodges the documents governed by the law into a part of Companies Register named Collection of documents, into a relevant branch concerning the incorporated commercial company. These documents are especially deeds of incorporation, establishing to a post of a company body member and other.

2.1.3 ORGANISATIONAL STRUCTURE

Organisational structure of each particular form of commercial company is prescribed by the Commercial Code. Each commercial company has its supreme body, consisting of company partners. Each particular form of commercial company has its governing body as well, i.e. a body acting on behalf of the company to third party, this body's acting is considered to be a personal acting of the company. The Commercial Code prescribes a control body, a supervisory board, to stock corporations as well. Limited liability company may facultatively establish a supervisory board, if the partners specify so in company's deed of incorporation. The supervisory board establishing is obligatory for public companies limited by shares.

All commercial companies' bodies' members should meet general requirements to discharge of office. These are age over 18, legal capacity, and without criminal record in accordance with trade law. The requirement of no criminal record is defined negatively, i.e. a person who does not meet this requirement is defined. Within the meaning of that, a person is not without criminal record, if He has been sentenced lawfully for:

a) a criminal offence committed intentionally, irrespective if separate or in combination of offences, and custodial sentence was inflicted for at least a year, or

b) a criminal offence committed intentionally, if not related to a), if the criminal offence was committed in connection with businessship, barring situation, when a legal fiction is applied and the person is considered to be not sentenced.

If a commercial company's body member candidate meets general requirements to discharge of the office of a commercial company's governing body member or a commercial company's supervisory board member, there mustn't be any obstacles and the person must be enabled to discharge his office. Commercial Code in its General part about commercial companies defines this. Obstacles, from the point of discharging the office, mean a state, when the person discharged any of comparable offices for a legal person, whose assets turned bankrupt. The same rule is applied, if an insolvency petition is denied for lack of assets. Persistence of the obstacle is limited and is not insuperable for commercial companies to set a particular person a governing body member or a supervisory body member. If commercial company's supreme body is informed about the obstacle and nevertheless voted the candidate as a body member or connames his membership, the person becomes, or stays, a legitimate company's body member. Details are given by the author of the text in the foregoing part about the Companies Register.

A person may be appointed or voted a commercial company's body member. Discharge of the function of a company body's member is ended by his suspension from office, resignation, upon agreement between the company and the partner, an obstruction of the discharge of the function appearance – without subsequent connameation of the person's function by the supreme company's body, by lapse of tenure, dissatisfying general requirements essential to discharge of the office, or by company's body member death.

Discharge of the company's body member office shouldn't be in form of employment relationship. If a contract of employment between the company and the company's body member is concluded, determining discharge of the company's body member office, it would be considered to be an invalid contractual relationship. The contractual relationship between the company's body member and the commercial company, consisting of mutual subjective rights and obligations of the relation parties, represents a pure commercial-law relationship. For this purpose, it is possible to conclude a so called contract of discharge of office. This contract should be connameed by the supreme body representing the party of the commercial company. There are no requirements prescribed by the Commercial Code. On the other hand, a necessity of the written form arises from the Commercial Code. Another provision of the Commercial Code prescribes, that if a contract of discharge of office should be concluded, provisions about a contract of mandate will be appropriately applied. If there is no contract concluded between a company's body member and the commercial company, the relationship should be qualified appropriately in accordance with legal regulations of the contract of mandatory. It arises from legal regulations of the contract of mandatory, or directly from contract of discharge of office, that company's body member is entitled to be remunerated adequately for the discharge of his office. However, although the company's body member is entitled to that, the commercial company may refuse to pay it in a case that the company's body member contributed to company's unfavourable economic results.

If prescribed by law or by a deed of incorporation that a governing body or a supervisory body should have more members, it is a collective body. As such, it makes decisions collectively, i.e. in the presence of at least over one half of the body members, which is by absolute majority of present members. Except for personal voting at the company's body meeting, deeds of incorporation may admit presence and voting through means of communication technology.

From the point of discharge of office and potential company's body member liability for incurred damage, law defines in open manner a basic requirement in terms of discharge of office quality. Each body member should discharge the office as so called an ordinary economist (meaning duly). This term is not defined by the Commercial Code and its content is left for practise, law interpretation and courts' practise. With time the term got certain definition characteristics, especially loyalty, secrecy, preference of company's interests to personal interests, carefulness and so on. If in relation with company's body member's actions damage occurs and the member did not act as an ordinary economist, the commercial company is liable for damage and obliged to recompense the aggrieved for it. The acting company's body member is in such a case a legal surety for fulfilling the commitment. The commercial company may as a regress claim compensatory damage from the acting company's body member. The compensatory obligation presumes that the acting company's body member did not act as an ordinary economist. The burden of proving is placed on a member of board of directors. He should prove that acted as an ordinary economist. The person exercising claim for damage only asserts amount of compensation for damage, turns attention to actions, which in his opinion are not in accordance with actions of an ordinary economist, proves causality between this action and damage occurrence. Culpability plays no role in commercial-law relations.

The Commercial Code, from all ways of winding-up of the office, focuses on resignation from office especially, i.e. one-sided legal deed of a company's body member, which results in winding-up of his company's body membership. A company's body member should notify the company's body (where He discharged the office) or the body where He was voted about his resignation from the office. A company's body member may announce the resignation at concerned body meeting, or may notify the resignation in written form to the company's body. If the resignation is announced at the meeting, discharge of the office expires within two months from the meeting. If the resignation is notified in another way, the discharge of the office terminates the day, when the concerned company's body debated, or should have debated, the resignation. The concerned company's body is the body, which voted the body member to his office, unless the deed of incorporation provides, that the concerned body is the body, which the resigning person is a member of. Postponement of the moment of the office winding-up till the debating, or a possibility of debating, by the concerned company's body brings the commercial company, i.e. its supreme body, a possibility to choose a new appropriate candidate for discharge of the office. As it is enough to debate the resignation for winding-up of the office, or a possibility to debate it, whereas resignation is a one-sided legal deed of a company's body member, it is not necessary to realise the debate. In a case that the resignation is debated, the result of the debate is not deciding for the discharge of office winding-up. From the moment of resignation notifying out of the concerned body meeting to the moment of discharge of the office winding-up there should not pass more than 3 months. After this period it is applied that the concerned company's body had possibility to debate the resignation, even in a case that the company's body was not validly convened during the period. The same is applied if the concerned body had a possibility to debate the resignation, was validly convened, but was not quorate.

Scope of particular commercial companies' bodies appears from the Commercial Code, alternatively from deeds of incorporation of a commercial company. The scope of the company's supreme body covers the most important decisions about company matters. That means especially decisions about contents of deed of incorporation alterations, company's bodies' members' election or voting off, registered capital change, connameation of actions done before company formation, decisions about companies' transformations and so on. The company's supreme body may extend the scope and cover other matters as well. The commercial company's supreme body holds proceedings at least once per year.

The scope of a governing body is in essence of two kinds. On one hand the governing body discharges so called "commercial management", on the other hand acts on behalf of the company to third party. Commercial management are actions within the company fulfilling company's businessial activities. Acting on behalf of the company is its personal acting, which means that legal consequences ascribed to the company directly. The governing body discharges permanent administration of a commercial company between company's supreme body's proceedingss and is responsible to the supreme body for its discharge of functioning. The scope of the functioning covers especially securing regular accounting procedures conducting, preparing businessial activities reports, company's assets state report, acting towards state administration etc.

The scope of a supervisory body is, as the name implies, supervision. A supervisory board supervises regular discharge of company's bodies' members' offices, controls regular conducting accounting procedures, reports to the general meeting, should affix its consent to certain governing body's decisions etc.

The Commercial Code regulates "ban on competition". It is related prior to commercial companies' bodies' members. The ban on competition means the company's body member must not:

- Be in the same or similar branch of business or enter into business relationship with the company,
- Mediate or arrange the company deals for other persons,

- Take part in businessship of another company as an unlimited partner or a controlling person of another person with the same or similar branch of business, and
- Discharge activities as a governing body or a member of a governing or another body of another legal person with the same or similar branch of business activities, except of concern.

If a company's body member violates the ban, the company may, but does not have to, demand compensation; transfer of benefits acquired by violating the ban on competition and acquired rights transfer from the company's body member to the company.

2.1.4 REGISTERED CAPITAL AND PARTNERS' INVESTMENTS

Although different opinions manifest themselves significantly, the dominating theory of registered capital in the Czech commercial law is about its guarantee intent. The guarantee function is, in accordance with the Czech commercial law, based on the fact, that the registered capital is a kind of a guarantee of at least the value of net assets of a commercial company expressed in monetary value.

Registered capital represents a monetary expression of monetary and non-monetary all partners' investments in total. It is necessary to enter the value of the registered capital to the Companies Register, in part recording information of a particular commercial company, to keep the function of a guarantee. As the registered capital is all partners' investments in total, the limited partnerships are obliged to register it (as limited partners are the partners obliged to invest), as well as limited liability companies and public companies limited by shares. The Commercial Code specifies the minimum value of the registered capital, as well as minimum partners' investments for particular types of commercial companies. The registered capital of limited partnerships amounts at least CZK 5,000, limited liability companies at least CZK 200,000, public companies limited by shares at least CZK 2,000,000, if incorporated without public offer of subscription of shares, and CZK 20,000,000, if incorporated with public offer of subscription of shares.

The Commercial Code prescribes different possibilities of registered capital amount change for limited liability companies and for public companies limited by shares. The amount of registered capital is one of the basic obligatory information incorporated in the Companies Register. Incorporation in the Companies Register is of a constitutive character, i.e. the change is realized at the moment of the incorporation. As above-mentioned, only limited partners of limited partnerships, partners of limited liability companies and shareholders of public companies limited by shares are obliged to investments. Partners of general partnership may grant voluntary investments. In such a case, this is not incorporated in the Companies Register. Subjects of investments may be monetary and non-monetary. Investments mean monetary means and other non-monetary means valuable in money in total that a partner pledges to invest into the registered company capital of a commercial company. It is necessary therefore to differentiate terms "investment" and "a subject of investment". Investment represents only monetary expression of all subjects of investments value; however a subject of investment represents a particular asset value granted to a commercial company.

Non-monetary investment may be any property valuable in money and usable in relation with subject of business of a commercial company. Investments in a form of partners labour or service providing are not allowed. Non-monetary subject of investment should be valued and the value should be entered in a Memorandum of Association and afterwards in the Companies Register as well. It is sufficient for personal commercial companies to value the non-monetary subjects of investments to make a partners agreement. On the other hand, limited liability companies and public companies limited by shares should value the non-monetary subjects of investments on the basis of expert opinion. The expert is appointed by a court for the particular valuation on the proposal of the commercial company. Expert's remuneration is financed by the commercial company, where the non-monetary subject of investment should be invested into the registered capital. The expert opinion describes the subject of investment, methods of evaluation applied and the value the expert evaluates the subject of investment. Memorandum of Association states the value of non-monetary investment and amount set off from the total value of the partner's investment to registered capital. Non-monetary investment should be redeemed before registered capital incorporation in the Companies Register. Investment rendered becomes company's assets. If it does not happen by force of circumstances, the partner is obliged to invest monetary valuable consideration instead of non-monetary subject of investment into the registered capital. If the value of non-monetary subject of investment lowers under the value that should be set off from the partner's investment to a commercial company during the time from the moment of evaluation till the company formation, eventually the moment of redemption, the partner is obliged to pay up the difference in money.

The Commercial Code distinguishes the moment of investment redemption and transfer of proprietary right to the subject of investment from a partner to a commercial company. The variance of both moments is emphasized during the process of commercial company incorporation and formation. During the process of commercial company incorporation and formation, it is necessary to evaluate the non-monetary subject of investment and the value should be stated in the Memorandum of Association, and afterwards the partner is obliged to redeem the investment. The fact, that the partner discharged the investment obligation should be proved to the court keeping the relevant Companies Register. Discharging the investment obligation, i.e. redeeming the investment, is necessary for commercial company incorporation in the Companies Register, i.e. for its formation. The investment is at least partially discharged during the time between company's incorporation and formation. The registered capital should be increased by the investment, however the commercial company does not legally exist at the moment, it does not have corporate personality, and it cannot come into posproceedings of subjects of investments. The company does not come into posproceedings of subjects of investments before its formation, i.e. at the moment of the company's incorporation in the Companies Register. Subjects of investments, posproceedings of which comes by recording in a special registration, e.g. real property recorded in the Land Registry, or subjects of rights of intellectual property.

Whilst non-monetary investments must be fully redeemed before commercial company formation, monetary investments should be partially redeemed in limits prescribed by law. One-member commercial companies are an exception, i.e. companies incorporated by one incorporator, as even their monetary investments should be fully redeemed before commercial company formation.

An administrator of investments appointed in Memorandum of Association administers the partners' investments before company's formation. One of the incorporators or a bank may be an administrator. The administrator connames partners' discharge of the investment obligation amd administers the investments till the moment the commercial company formed comes into posproceedings of the investments. After its formation the administrator transfers redeemed investments together with fruit and benefits, all documents and other tools needed for investments usage, eventually for coming into posproceedings with them. In a case of monetary investments, a special bank account in a bank is kept for the purpose by the administrator of investments.

Monetary investments are redeemed at the moment of money transfer to an administrator of investments or to a special bank account, opened for this purpose. Non-monetary investments in form of movables are redeemed at the moment of their handing over to an administrator of investments. If a real property presents a non-monetary investment, it is necessary at the moment the real property is ceded to sign a so called declaration of investment, which is consequently a legal title for a record in the Land Register in favour of the newly formed commercial company. In case of other non-monetary investments, it is necessary to conclude an agreement with the company, represented by an administrator of investments and his signature, together with the subject of investment handing over.

2.1.5 SHARE

Partner's interest in a commercial company is represented by his share in the company. A share may be defined from a qualitative or quantitative view. The first, i.e. a qualitative, view is based on partner's rights and obligations related with the share. From the qualitative point of view, it is a degree of partner's interest in a company, i.e. the extent of the share. The Commercial Code specifies the interest to the form of a business share in the case of a limited liability company. A Public company limited by shares is exceptional as the interest is only in this type of commercial company represented by a commercial paper – a share.

There are rights and obligations of monetary and non-monetary character related to a share. The essential monetary obligation is usually investment obligation. An essential non-monetary obligation is loyalty to a commercial company. An essential non-monetary right is the right to participate in a company's supreme body meeting through the right of vote. An essential monetary right is the right of share of profits of the company, settlement share, or share in the liquidation surplus.

The supreme company's body decides about contingent profit share payment after proportional obligatory share from profit from the last accounting period is transferred to the company's funds. A partner obtains right of settlement share in a company in a case of different winding-up of his interest in a company than through a share cessation, however the commercial company still existing. Settlement share is a financial payment of a share value at the date of the partner's membership winding-up in the commercial company. The amount of the share is assessed on the basis of final accounts made till the moment of the partner's membership winding-up, from the value of equity capital.

The last alternative of a share is a share in the liquidation surplus. In connection with commercial company dissolution, the company is put into liquidation for one of reasons prescribed by law in a case, when the commercial company is in black from accounting and economic view. A person appointd as a liquidator administers the liquidation. The liquidation target is to finish commercial company activities, close businessship, settle all debts to creditors of the commercial company, and to collect all claims of the liquidated commercial company.

After all debts and receivables of the liquidated commercial company settling, the liquidator prepares the statement of liquidation process, calculates the liquidation surplus as a net proprietary balance of the liquidated commercial company and proposes a way of allotment of the liquidation surplus. The proposal of liquidation surplus allotment specifies a share from the liquidation surplus proposed for each partner.

2.1.6 COMMERCIAL COMPANY'S WINDING-UP AND DISSOLUTION

The Commercial Code differentiates commercial company's winding-up and dissolution, as well as incorporation and formation. A commercial company may be wound-up only in prescribed ways. A commercial company is not dissolved till the moment of its erasure from the Companies Register. There is a time lag between a commercial company winding-up and dissolution, the time lag is intended for commercial company's rights and obligations settling in relation to third party or the partners. A commercial company may be wound-up with or without liquidation. Winding-up without liquidation means winding-up of a commercial company, which has a legal successor. This typically happens in case of transformation of commercial companies, which presents a content of a special chapter. Liquidation is not required also in other exceptional situations specified in the Commercial Code, especially in relation with insolvency proceedings.

A commercial company winding-up appears by:

- Expiration of the time for which it was formed,
- Attainment of objectives for which it was formed,
- The day stated in partners' decision of company's body decision about company's dissolution, otherwise the day, when the decision was accepted, if the company is wound-up with liquidation,
- The day stated in judicial decision about company's dissolution, otherwise the day when judicial decision becomes legally effective,
- The day stated in partners' decision or company's body decision, if the company is wound-up as a result of a company merger, equity transfer to a partner or as a result of division, otherwise the day when the decision was accepted,

- Cancellation of bankruptcy after satisfying a resolution about the liquidation surplus allotment or by cancellation of bankruptcy for absolutely unsatisfactory property of the debtor.

Anyone, who decided about the commercial company dissolution and putting the company into liquidation, has the right to appoint the person of liquidator. Commercial company's dissolution with liquidator is recorded in the Companies Register, as well as the person of liquidator. Anyone, who decided about the commercial company dissolution and putting the company into liquidation, has also usually the right to remove the person of a liquidator and appoint another person for the position. The same authority has, on certain conditions, right to revoke own decision about the commercial company winding-up and putting into liquidation. The person of liquidator is usually appointd from governing body's members or from partners.

In connection with company winding-up and its subsequent liquidation or insolvency proceedings, a situation may appear that there would be two bodies operating side by side concurrently, authorised to act on behalf of the company to third party. A liquidator or insolvency administrator nomination does not eliminate the governing body operating. When a liquidator is appointd by a commercial company, He acquires a scope of authority in limits necessary for discharge of the office. For the purpose only those tasks are necessary, which lead to commercial company activities winding-up, its liquidation and dissolution. In other respects the authority of the governing body remains untouched. If the liquidator learns during liquidation that conditions for insolvency proceedings initiation are met, He is obligated to file such a motion. At the moment of insolvency administrator nomination, the authority of the governing body henceforth remains untouched, but again in limits of the scope of authority that did not pass over to the insolvency administrator.

If a court makes decision about the commercial company winding-up, it may do so only for following reasons:

- No general meeting was held in last two years; or company's bodies, which period of office or all their members' period of office had expired more than one year ago, were not elected last year, unless provided otherwise; or the company is not active more than two years,

- The company loses authorisation to carry on business,
- Prerequisites required by law for company formation disappear, or if the company is not able to carry on business for its partners insurmountable conflicts,
- The company breaches the duty to set up a surplus fund,
- The company breaches the duty to practise the scope of a special activity only through persons specially authorised for the scope of the activity,
- The company does not carry its duty to sell a part of the company or to divide the company, the duty placed by the Competition authority in accordance with a special legal regulation.

In all above-mentioned cases, the court gives respite to obviate the reason for its winding-up. If the company reacts to the call and obviates the reason for potential dissolution, the court subsequently does not proceed with the legal proceedings and the company's winding-up is not finished.

On the other hand, it may happen that a company is formed although the basic conditions for its formation are not met. In such a case, it is not possible to sue for designation the company was not formed. However, the court may declare the invalidity of the company in following cases:

- No Memorandum of Association or deed of incorporation were concluded or the prescribed form was not abode,
- The subject of business (activities) is unauthorised or is contrary to the public order,
- Data about the name name, or the partners investments, or the sum of the registered capital, if prescribed by law; or the subject of business (activities) are missing in the Memorandum of Association, or the deed of incorporation, or the Articles of Association,

- The provisions of minimum investment pay were not observed,
- All company forming partners are legally incapable,
- The number of partners forming the company is lower than two, contravening the regulations.

If the court adjudged invalidity of the commercial company for above-mentioned reasons, the commercial company comes into liquidation and after its winding-up; it will be deleted from the register, which means its dissolution. This adjudication does not affect partners' investment obligation, if they did not fully discharge their investment obligation till the moment of court adjudication of invalidity of the company; nor affects legal relationships.

As above-mentioned, a wound-up company comes into liquidation in a case that its value stays in black economically and has no successor in title. Information about coming into liquidation and the person of liquidator are entered in the Companies Register. Information about the fact that the company is in liquidation becomes a part of the commercial company's trade description as well and it the trade description of the commercial company, together with "in liquidation" addendum, is used also when acting towards third parties. In a case, the commercial company was wound-up on the basis of the company's supreme body's decision; the governing body appoints the person of liquidator.

If a commercial company was wound-up on the basis of its supreme body's decision, the governing body appoints the liquidator. In a case, that the commercial company was wound-up for adjudication, the court appoints the liquidator. The one who appoints the liquidator, makes decisions about his suspension and remuneration. Except from commercial company's liquidation the liquidator accomplishes claims filing, debts payments, acting towards third persons, including courts and the Companies Register; and the liquidator is authorised to conclude new contracts. However, there is a requirement that the contracts concluded by the liquidator should bring current legal relationships to a close, or utilize the current commercial company's property, or keeping its value. This means contracts such as contracts of hire/lease etc.

The liquidator's activities after nomination begin with drawing up following documentation:

- Final accounts on the date of the day before the date of commercial company's dissolution,
- Liquidation balance sheet on the date of commercial company's coming into liquidation,
- Inventory of commercial company's property,
- Liquidation announcement.

Whilst the character the first three documents is informative especially for the liquidator and partners, the liquidation announcement is important information especially for creditors. For this reason the liquidator informs all known creditors about the commercial company coming into liquidation and as other creditors may exist, hitherto unknown, makes a liquidation announcement through the Commercial bulletin. After the first, informative stage, the liquidator starts actions leading to commercial company's activities winding-up and its liquidation.

Evaluation of the liquidation process, results evaluation, and subsequent liquidation balance allotment represent the final stage of liquidation. After conducting all acts of commercial company's liquidation, the liquidator sets up following documents:

- Commercial company's liquidation process report,
- A proposal of liquidation balance allotment among the partners of the company,
- Final accounts on the date of the proposal of liquidation balance allotment draw up.

The liquidator submits the mentioned documents for approval to the partners. If any of the partners doubts his share on the liquidation balance is correct, He may apply to the court for a review. The right may be asserted only within three months from consideration of the proposal of liquidation balance allotment. The liquidation balance allotment should not be started until all known creditors are paid off. If the liquidator is not successful in converting some property into money, the property is offered the creditors as a settlement of debt.

The liquidator again submits a report about the property disposal for approval to the partners. The liquidator makes final accounts on the date of the report compiling.

The process of liquidation finishes by allotment of liquidation balance, eventually of the property comprising the balance, among the partners, or creditors. The liquidator cannot file a proposal to erasure the commercial company from the Companies Register, which means its dissolution, until 30 days from finishing liquidation. The liquidator secures archiving of the dissolved commercial company's documentation at the same time. If any property appears after the commercial company's dissolution additionally, the competent court, managing the Companies Register, may resume the commercial company's existence and renew the liquidation as well. After performing all necessary acts of liquidation renewal, the court deletes the commercial company from the Companies Register again.

2.1.7 COMMERCIAL COMPANIES' TRANSFORMATION

Commercial companies' transformations are not regulated by the Commercial Code, but by a special act. Commercial company's transformation usually means at least one company's winding-up and its property assumption by another, successor, commercial company, including the rights and obligations from labour-law relations. Exception to above-mentioned is represented by a company's transformation, where only one company does not wind-up, but only transforms its organisation structure and partners' legal relations through the legal form transformation. The company transforms from a limited liability company to a Public company limited by shares for example.

A commercial company's transformation may be realised by following:

- Merger,
- Division,
- Registered capital transfer to a partner, or
- Legal form transformation.

Merger means at least two commercial companies consolidate into one successor company. The merger may be realised between two commercial companies residing in the Czech Republic, but it may be one domestic and one foreign commercial company as well. Commercial companies' transformation in form of merger may be lead in two ways. On one hand, the merger may be realised by absorption, but on the other hand, it may be by formation of a new company as well. A special act characterises the merger by absorption as a company's transformation, while during this process at least one company's dissolution comes, the dissolution being preceded by the company's winding-up without liquidation, and subsequently its assets, including the rights and obligations from labour-law relations, pass to the successor company. That means that in case of a merger, one of the companies involved winds-up and its assets pass to another company. The merger by formation of a new company differs from the merger by absorption only in dissolving all companies involved, while the successor company is a newly formed company.

There are only several legal ways how a company may be transformed in form of division, i.e.:

1. division with new companies' formation,
2. division by absorption,
3. combination of both mentioned forms,
4. splitting with new companies' formation,
5. division by splitting off and merger by absorption,
6. combination of above mentioned forms.

First, let's mention the division with new companies' formation. A special act defines this form of transformation as a splitting company's winding-up without liquidation and its subsequent dissolution related to assets, including rights and obligations from labour-law relations passing to successor companies. These are newly formed companies. A commercial company may divide, forming new companies, while a joint stock company or a limited liability company may become a successor company. The result of a company with new companies' formation is the divided company's dissolution and its assets, including registered capital, investments and contingent business interests, passing to the newly formed companies. As a consequence of that the newly formed company may acquire interest in a limited liability company.

As a result, the newly formed company may acquire an interest in a limited liability company. This is a case of derivative acquisition. The author deems possible a business interest division and its parts subsequent transfer to a newly formed company. The author considers possible business interest in posproceedings of dissolved company division and its parts subsequent transfer to the newly formed company.

Division of a company by absorption is based on dissolved company division and its capital transfer by absorption to an existing company. Only existing companies acquire divided company's capital. The existing companies may derivatively acquire an interest in a limited liability company, or, if they had been a business interest owner in the same company, they may increase their interest in the limited liability company by business shares consolidation.

Division of a company by splitting off with new companies' formation and division by splitting off by absorption are based on a certain part of an existing company severance, while this part of the company separated becomes a new company, or its separated part will be incorporated into an existing company in form of a merger. In respect of the nature of these transformation forms, the comment of two above-mentioned forms of division may be applied, as in relation with an interest incorporation the comment would be similar as in the case of division with new companies' formation and division by absorption.

Other forms of company transformation in form of division are divisions by combinations of above-mentioned forms. It appears from the term of transformation in a form of division that the dissolved company is dissolved without liquidation and its assets transfer subsequently, including the rights and obligations from labour-law relations, to another company. The author purposedly did not use the term of a successor company, as the term would not be accurate. In such a case of company transformation, the capital partly transfers to newly formed companies and partly to successor companies, i.e. existing companies.

The principle of capital transfer to a partner is company's winding-up without liquidation and its subsequent dissolution with capital transfer to a partner at the same time.

The principle of legal form transformation, in contrast to most of above-mentioned companies' transformations, is not one or more companies' dissolution, nor the subsequent dissolved company's assets transfer. Legal form transformation should be understood only as company's legal relations transformation and related partners' legal status transformation. This form of transformation is therefore related to just one commercial company. The company is, after its form transformation entry into Companies Register, within the meaning of its legal existence the same as before the transformation realisation. After the company's transformation entry into the Companies Register comes into effect, only its legal form changes. The above-mentioned interpretation of the principle of this form of company's transformation is a reflection of the principle of legal person continuity.

Commercial companies' transformation process is relatively extended, demanding and strictly formalised. Common features may be noticed in all transformation forms in general contour. The process may be generally and simplified divided into following stages:

- Commercial company's decision about its transformation,
- Decisive date of the transformation,
- Transformation project creation,
- Information about commercial company's transformation realisation intent and transformation project publication,
- Initial final accounts and balance sheet execution and their verification by an auditor,
- Transformation report discharged by governing bodies of all concerned commercial companies,
- Expert valuation of concerned commercial companies' assets,
- The transformation project authorisation – decision about transformation,

- Entering the transformation into the Companies Register, which is the moment of commercial company's transformation realisation,
- Final accounts setting up and verification – after the transformation.

The purport of final accounts should be on one hand control for partners of concerned commercial companies, on the other hand for court's control of financial sufficiency of the commercial company during the transformation, in relation with transformation form planned and economical values and ratios of the successor commercial company. The record date is within the meaning the date since when commercial company's conduct has been ascribed to the successor commercial company.

Final accounts verification and expert's report about the transformed commercial company's assets are important for the court control, as well as for protection of partners, who disagreed with the transformation and may terminate their interest in the successor commercial company and may acquire recompense for their share from the company. At the same time, the account ratios, their auditor's verification and expert's opinion should have informative and protective character for potential creditors of the transformed commercial company. From this point of view, it is important to publish the commercial company's intention to realise its transformation and publish basic specifications of the transformation. Basic specifications and the intention to realise the transformation are published by the commercial company by way of entering the transformation project into the Collection of legal documents of the Companies Register, and by way of publishing the project with an announcement about the transformation planned in the Commercial bulletin. The transformation project is published at the beginning of the transformation process and the same text is subsequently, after all necessary stages realisation, authorised by the supreme body of the commercial company. Afterwards the project of transformation is entered into the Companies Register on the basis of the authorised transformation project. The transformation entry is of constitutive character again, i.e. the transformation takes effect at the moment of commercial company's entry into the Companies Register.

The project of transformation consists of basic information and planned results of the commercial company's transformation, especially:

- Transformed commercial companies' identification,
- Record date of commercial company's transformation,
- Data about structure of taken-over assets of dissolved commercial companies and their impact on successor commercial company's assets,
- Information about the organisation structure changes and alternatively about future commercial company's bodies' members,
- Successor commercial company's deed of incorporation proposal, etc.

Not only transformation project publishing, final accounts setting up and their auditor's verification and expert's concerned commercial companies' assets evaluation, but governing bodies' of concerned commercial companies report about the transformation planned. The report should consist of especially:

- Grounds of business interests or shares exchange rate, if they should be exchanged,
- Grounds of registered capital investments amount and possible additional payments to even up and measures in favour of particular classes of commercial papers' owners – commercial papers issued by a concerned commercial company or cooperative,
- Description of troubles that occurred during evaluation for exchange rate of business interests or shares purpose, or an information that no troubles occurred,
- Partners' or members' economical and legal status changes,
- Extent of liability changes of commercial companies' partners or cooperatives' members, or some of them, if the extent of liability of the partners or members, or some of them, changes,

- Transformation impact on creditors of the commercial company or a cooperative, especially from the point of their claims recoverability

Each commercial company's transformation should be authorised by the transformed commercial company's supreme body by qualified majority of votes. The transformation becomes effective at the moment of entry into the Companies Register. As a commercial company's transformation influences the rights of partners/members fundamentally, law admits the dissenting partner/member to resign from the transformed commercial company under certain circumstances, and acquire from the commercial company financial compensation for his interest, based on expert's evaluation. At first, the partner/member should notify of his dissent from the transformation in public to enable his resignation from the transformed commercial company. The partner/member willing to resign from the commercial company must endeavour to prevent the commercial company's transformation. The partner/member must take part in supreme body's meeting, which should decide about the transformation, i.e. authorise the transformation project, and he must vote against the transformation authorisation during the meeting and the fact must be mentioned in the notarial record drawn up by the commercial company's supreme body. If the transformation project is authorised, the partner/member should notify the company of his decision to resign from the commercial company within 30 days from the transformation authorisation.

2.1.8 Business Grouping

Grouping of at least two businesses – in inferior and superior relationship - is considered a concern, at least one business being inferior person in authority to unitary management of another business, comporting as a superior person. The business, in limits of concern, should be understood also as a business of a natural person, which is worth noticing. Naturally such a natural person may act only as a superior person. The superior relationship may be based on legaly or factually. The reason of legal superiority is especially a control deed; however, the reason for factual superiority is majority of voting rights acquisition, personal link of a considerable number of companies' bodies' members, etc. In practise, the difference is in extent of the superior person influence over the superior person.

In a case of the factual concern, the superior person may not influence bodies' decision-making of the inferior person directly, as they should discharge their function duly, which is an obligation not to the superior person, but to the inferior person, as they are its body's members. The superior person may therefore influence only their appointment to the office, or removal.

The legal/contractual concern is based on managing through a control deed, which clearly presumes the inferior person's bodies should be obliged to respect superior person's will and instructions. Damage done so to the inferior person must be made good. Even in a case the superior person makes inferior person's bodies' members act in a way damaging the inferior person, the superior person is obliged to make good the damage. Regardless of this obligation, the body's members, who did not discharge their office duly, are responsible for the damage to the company and are obliged by legal liability for company's obligations towards third party. Law regulates particularly contractual concerns, the main subject represented by third party protection and concern companies' partners' protection. One of the most important instruments are primarily obligations of publishing character, meaning written report about interrelations between the superior person and inferior persons; the report control within the companies, or by an auditor, and subsequent publishing in the Collection of documents of the Companies Register.

Another way of controlling differentiation may be direct and indirect control. Direct control means immediate control of the inferior company through right to vote exercising. Indirect control means controlling through another person. Another criterion of differentiation may be so called "setting up a concern" of pyramidal, radial or circulation structure. In a case of the pyramidal concern, the parent company controls several subsidiary companies and through them so called "subsubsidiary" companies. On the other hand, the parent company controls several subsidiary companies without other level of control in a radial structured concern. The circulation structured concern means a mutual control circle of concern companies. Third parties' and partners' standing out protection is guaranteed by control contract, surplus transfer contact, and alternatively report about interrelations between the superior and inferior persons publication. The correctness of data given in the report about relations, made by governing bodies, should be affirmed by supervisory bodies, eventually also by an auditor. The report publishing is realised by the Collection of documents of the Companies Register. The report should be a real reflection of the concern and interrelations among concern companies.

Assets transferability limitation is very important for relations within the concern. The limitation relates not only to persons forming the concern, but to contractual relationship between the company and a shareholder, or persons acting in accordance with it. These are persons acting being mutually aware of the target to acquire, pass, or exercise voting right in a particular person, or dispose of them to assert collective influence on management or running the business of the person; or governing body voting, or its members, or majority of its members, or majority of supreme body members' voting, or another influence on particular person's behaviour. Besides above mentioned general definition, persons acting in accordance are, based on an irrebuttable legal presumption, considered also particularly:

- Legal person and its governing body or its member, persons under their direct control, supervisory body's member,
- Superior person and its inferior persons,
- Persons controlled by the same superior person,
- Persons forming one concern,
- Limited liability company and its partners or just its partners.

Defining persons forming a concen and persons acting in accordance is necessary to prevent fatal error of property transfers among concern members. The above mentioned provision consists of two kinds of limitations. At first, it limits possibility to conclude a credit contract, a loan contract, an obligations security contract, or gratuitous deed of company's peroperty in favour of its bodies' members or other persons authorised to act on behalf of the company or persons close to them.

Concluding such a contract is possible only if based on general meeting approval and in limits of standard conditions of commercial relations. It is not necessary to keep these strict rules only in a case of loans, credit or security of an inferior company granted by a superior person.

The second separate group of facts limiting contractual relationship are property transfers limitations between the commercial company and above mentioned persons, the commercial company and its inferior company, a founder, a shareholder, a person in acting in accordance with it, or a person forming the concern with it; if the value of the transferred property, or consideration, exceeds one tenth of subscribed registered capital. In such a case, the transfer is possible only if based on an expert's opinion, the expert being appointed by a court, for a price determined by the expert's opinion. If the property is acquired within 3 years from the company incorporation, the general meeting approval is necessary as well, however, following legal exceptions are allowed. A practical, frequently used, exception is a situation, when the transfer is realised in limits of common commercial relations. In limits of a concern, the concern reaction reflecting the market requirements is obstructed by the necessity of the expert's opinion. The general meeting approves the transfer during a relatively short period after its necessity finding. It becomes possible not to keep the period for general meeting convening given by law, when 100% of partners/shareholders are present and all of them waive the right of early general meeting convening through declaring they will not institute legal proceedings for nonvalidity of ordinary resolution. This procedure became an important part of concern companies' practise, and it may be appreciated that even the court practise tends to this practical solution in this respect, turning away from frequent formalism in Companies Register matters. The loss of time results from the necessity of an expert's appointment by court, regional court has material competence, locally a court competent for the place of the registered office. Although the court reacts relatively quickly after filling a proposal, the delivery time, time to render a decision and subsequent delivery time, that all means a time lag. There must be made provisions for the time needed for expert's opinion elaboration. It becomes possible to realise the transfer only after an expert's appointment becomes effective, based on the expert's opinion. Common practise tends to make the process more rapid, e.g. if the proposal for an expert's appointment is delivered personally, court fee payed at the same time; the resolution appointing an expert, concerning the company, may be subsequently collected personally, provided that all the concerned waive the right of appeal at the same moment. It has become a common practise to consult the expert about evaluation before his appointment proposing and the expert may start his work in advance, before his appointment. It is necessary to realise the transfers in limits of common commercial relations to make the above mentioned exception applicable. However, there is no clear boundary between actions of common commercial relations and actions beyond. Professional literature inferred that actions accomplishing the scope of business activities are in limits of common commercial relations. In any case it will be necessary to analyse each particular situation separately with respect to factual circumstances; consideration and evaluation of a particular judge being essential. It is recommended, for practical reasons, to bring a row of less significant acts during longer period than to bring one voluminous significant act at one stroke. If the formal process is not observed, it is sanctioned by absolute invalidity of such an act. In a case of a contractual concern, or a factual concern formed by voting rights or personal union of companies' bodies, the relation becomes quite clear and the need of observing the prescribed process increases.

2.2 PERSONAL COMPANIES

A general partnership and a limited partnership are personal companies. Personal companies are typical for the personal liability of the partners for the company's payables, for their presumed active participation in the company's events and activities and usually for the absence of the partners' capital contribution obligation. The general partnership is a clear form of a personal company in the above sense. With regard to the capital contribution obligation of the limited partners, who are one of the two types of partners in this company form, their limited liability for the company's payables up to the amount of their unpaid capital contribution and their not required participation in the company's activities, the limited partnership is not a clear form of a personal commercial company. With regard to the fact that the second group of partners, who are called general partners, meets all the characteristics of personal companies, the limited partnership is described as a general partnership with certain elements of capital companies.

2.2.1 GENERAL COMMERCIAL PARTNERSHIP

The general partnership is a clear form of a personal company. This means that the partners do not have a capital contribution obligation, they are liable for the company's payables with their total assets, they personally participate in the company's activities. The general partnership must have at least two partners, who have the same rights and obligations pursuant to law. In relation to third parties the general partnership acts under its own company name, i.e. the name recorded in the Companies Register. The company name of the general partnership consists of 'a stem', i.e. a name selected by the partners, and an end which represents the legal form of this company. The end can be formed in one of the following ways:

- veřejná obchodní společnost [general partnership],
- veř. obch. spol. [gen. part.],
- v.o.s. [g.p.]

Similarly as other companies a general partnership is formed by a Memorandum of Association and is incorporated upon the registration of this company in the Companies Register. The Memorandum of Association must be in writing with officially authenticated signatures of the partners. The mandatory essentials of the Memorandum of Association include:

- company name and registered office of the company,
- specification of the partners by a company or business name and registered office of a juristic person or a name and address of a natural person,
- company's area of business.

The petition for the registration of a general partnership in the Companies Register is to be signed by all partners and the Memorandum of Association and other appendices required by law are to be appended to it.

The governing body of the general partnership consists of all the partners. Each partner possesses both components of activities of a governing body, i.e. acting in relation to third parties and business management. The Commercial Code allows the partners, in the

Memorandum of Association, to restrict these directing powers of some of the partners, or to entrust only some, or even one of the partners with business management and entitlement to act in relation to third parties. That selected person performs the entrusted activity according to principles set by the partners in the Memorandum of Association.

The supreme body of the general partnership is all the partners while each partner has one vote. The partners carrying on business management are bound by decisions of the company's supreme body. The supreme body decides on the most significant issues of the company's life. Its competence includes, in particular, the following:

- decision on an amendment to the Memorandum of Association,
- decision to entrust a partner with business management or governing activities, decision on principles of these activities and the possible revocation of this entrusting,
- right to request information on all company issues from the partner entrusted with business management,
- decision on an amendment to the Memorandum of Association leading to the accession of another partner to the company, or on the leaving of one of the existing partners from the company,
- decision to eliminate the non-competition clause in case of one of the partners, i.e. to allow him to pursue a competing activity,
- financial statements approval.

As mentioned above, the partners do not have a capital contribution obligation. However, the Commercial Code does not hinder the possibility for the partners to undertake to provide capital contribution in the Memorandum of Association.

The fundamental rights of the partners include, in particular:

- right to participate in the decision making process in the company by voting,
- exercise of business management and right to recall the entrusting with business management,

- exercise of governing activity and right to resign from this function,
- right to a profit share,
- right to a share of a liquidation balance,
- right to a settlement share in case of termination of a partner's participation in the company,
- right to bring an action for damage against a partner who is liable for damage in relation to the company,
- right to request information on all company issues from the partner entrusted with business management, to check information contained there and in case of need to authorise an auditor or a tax advisor to audit the information,
- right to request from other partners adequate compensation for performance he provided on grounds of liability,
- right to propose to a court for it to wind up the company on governing grounds, etc.

The fundamental obligations of the partners include, in particular:

- obligation to carry out one's activities with due professional and fiduciary diligence,
- provision of capital contribution only if the Memorandum of Association provides for that obligation,
- if a partner is entrusted with business management, then he is obligated to provide partners, on request, with all information on events in the company,
- obligation to contribute to the payment of the company's loss equally with other partners,
- obligation to observe the non-competition clause,
- guarantee the company's payables, even after the termination of the partner's participation in the company; however, in that case he is liable only for the payables coming into existence during his presence in the company, etc.

The rights and obligations can be provided for in the Memorandum of Association in derogation of the law but within the governing limits.

The partner's participation in the general partnership is terminated upon:

- his leaving effected through an amendment to the Memorandum of Association,
- removal of the partner by a court decision upon a motion of the company on the ground of a repeated violation of his obligations despite the company's invitation to remedy the situation and a warning on the possibility of a motion for his removal from the company,
- partner's death while the heir of his share in the general partnership can recall his participation within three months of the final acquisition of the company share,
- recall of the participation in the company by a partner who acquired his share by inheritance,
- winding-up of the general partnership.

The general partnership is dissolved upon its striking off from the Companies Register. However, the dissolution is preceded by its winding-up in consequence of a decision on the bankruptcy concerning the company's assets or winding-up without a liquidation (i.e. with the transfer of assets to a legal successor) or with a liquidation. In addition to the general reasons for the winding-up of a company the Commercial Code provides for several special reasons for the winding-up of a general partnership; in general attention can be drawn to the following ones, in particular:

- termination of the partner's participation for any reason (death, removal, bankruptcy declaration, execution or enforcement of a decision affecting the partner's share, incapacitation or restriction of his legal capacity, loss of prerequisites of a partner of a general partnership, etc.),
- other reasons provided for in the Memorandum of Association,
- court decision upon a partner's motion on the ground that any of the partners seriously violates his obligations or that the company is not able to achieve the purpose for which it was formed.

2.2.2 LIMITED PARTNERSHIP

Halfway between personal and capital companies lies a limited partnership. The limited partnership has at least two partners and each of them represents one of the two types of partners. The partners are limited and general partners. While general partners are in an almost identical position as partners in a general partnership, the position of limited partners is close to the legal position of members of a limited liability company. Limited partners are obligated to provide capital contribution, they are liable for company's payables up to the amount of their unpaid capital contribution registered in the Companies Register and they are not necessarily required to participate personally in the activities of the limited partnership. For the above reasons the limited partnership is considered to be a personal company but with significant features of capital companies. The ambiguous nature of this form of company which is rather halfway between a general partnership and a limited liability company is also reflected in the provisions governing this form of company in the Commercial Code. This is because the provisions are rather brief. The text concerning the limited partnership can be brief because of a reference provision according to which provisions on the general partnership shall apply to the limited partnership as a whole, provisions on the limited liability company shall apply to the legal position of limited partners. Therefore the passage concerning the limited partnership contains only differences from both groups of provisions referred to.

The limited partnership too is incorporated upon its registration in the Companies Register after a motion has been filed which is signed by all partners and all appendices required by regulations are attached to it. The limited partnership is formed upon concluding a Memorandum of Association between at least two partners, of whom one must be a limited partners and one must be a general partner. While the Commercial Code does not provide for any special requirements regarding limited partners, general partners must satisfy, like partners in a general partnership, general requirements for exercising a trade licence and in their case there may not be obstacles to an exercise of a trade licence. After the payment of the capital contribution and the registration of this fact in the Companies Register the limited partners do not guarantee the company's payables. A limited partner would be liable in a larger extent, same as a general partner, only in case he enters into an agreement on behalf of the company without an authorisation. The general partners are liable for the company's payables with all their assets. The Memorandum of Association must be in writing with officially authenticated signatures of the partners. The mandatory essentials of the Memorandum of Association include:

- company name and registered office of the company,
- specification of the partners by a company or business name and registered office of a juristic person or a name and address of a natural person,
- area of business,
- specification as to which partners are general partners and which are limited partners,
- amount of capital contribution of each limited partner (at least CZK 5,000).

The company name of the limited partnership consists of a stem selected by the partners in the Memorandum of Association and an end describing the company's legal form. The end can have one of the following forms:

- komanditní společnost [limited partnership],
- kom. spol. [lim. part.],
- k.s. [l.p.]

The supreme body of the limited partnership is all the partners again. Each partner has one vote. The supreme body's competence includes, in particular:

- decision on an amendment to the Memorandum of Association,
- approval of financial statements,
- decision to wind up the company, etc.

The governing body of the limited partnership are the general partners. They are entrusted with company's business management too.

The fundamental rights of the partners include, in particular:

- right to participate in the company's activities by exercising the voting right,
- right to a profit share which is shared between the company and the general partners equally while the profit falling to the company is shared by the limited partners,
- general partners' right to perform business management and to act on behalf of the company in relation to third parties,
- limited partners' right to transfer their share in the limited partnership,
- limited partners' right to request information on all company issues, to consult the provided documents and to check information in them, or to authorise an auditor to check it,
- limited partners' right to a counterpart of the financial statements,
- right to a payment of a settlement share,
- right to a payment of a share of a liquidation balance.

The fundamental obligations of the partners include, in particular:

- limited partners' obligation to pay the capital contribution,
- general partners' obligation to furnish information and documents on the events occurring in the company to the limited partners upon their request,
- general partners' obligation to observe the non-competition clause,
- general partners' obligation to settle the company's loss,
- limited partners' liability up to the amount of their unpaid capital contribution and in the same extent as general partners if they act on behalf of the company without an authorisation.

The limited partner is not entitled to leave the company. If his participation ends in another way, that does not mean the winding-up of the company. If all limited partners' participation ends, the general partners can decide to change the legal form to a general partnership. This is because upon the end of all limited partners' participation the company no longer satisfies the requirements for the setting up and existence of a limited partnership but satisfies the conditions for the setting up and existence of a general partnership. If only one partner is remaining in the company he is entitled to decide on the transfer of assets to a partner within a lapse period [a right ceases to exist if not exercised during such period – translator's note]. In this way the last partner in the limited partnership assumes all the assets of the wound-up company and its activities.

2.3 STOCK CORPORATIONS

Stock corporations are a limited liability company and a public company limited by shares. Stock corporations may be characterised as companies, where partners, in principle, are not liable for company's obligations, they are not supposed to be necessarily active in the company, as the company should be managed by professional management; and the partners are obliged to invest. A limited partnership has some common features with stock corporations, but on the other hand, a limited liability company has some distinctive features of personal commercial companies. Within the meaning of that a limited liability company's maximum number of members is 50. Members of this commercial company are liable to the amount of aggregate of all unpaid investmentsof all members, registered by the Companies Register. A public company limited by shares is a clear form of a stock corporation. Shareholders are not limited in number, they are not supposed to be active in the company, and from their position of shareholders they are not liable for company's obligations.

2.3.1 LIMITED LIABILITY COMPANY

A limited liability company is the most recent type of all traditional types of companies. It is a capital company with features of personal companies. This company form can be formed by a single member, or during the existence of this company all the shares can be united in the hands of a single member. The maximum number of members is 50. However, one person can be a sole member in a maximum of three limited liability companies. The company is obligated to have a registered capital which is composed of a sum of cash values of contributions of all members. The nature of a capital company is confirmed by the obligatory creation of a reserve fund. This fund has a value of at least 10% of the registered capital. The reserve fund can be used for the settlement of the company's loss, in particular.

The limited liability company is formed upon a conclusion of a Memorandum of Association. It has to be in writing in the form of a notarial record. The mandatory essentials of the Memorandum of Association include, in particular:

- company name and registered office of the company,
- specification of the partners by a company or business name and registered office of a juristic person or a name and address of a natural person,
- area of business (activity),
- amount of the registered capital and the amount of capital contribution of each member including the way of and time limit for the payment of the capital contribution,
- names and addresses of the first Managing Directors of the company and the manner in which they act on behalf of the company,
- names and addresses of the members of the first Supervisory Board, if established,
- specification of the manager of capital contributions,
- other information required by this Act.

The limited liability company is also incorporated upon its registration in the Commercial Register. The motion is to be signed by all Managing Directors of the company. The counterpart of the notarial record of the Memorandum of Association and other enclosures required by the regulations are to be attached to the motion for the registration. The name of the limited liability company is composed of a stem and an end. The end represents the form of the company and can take one of the following forms:

- společnost s ručením omezeným [limited liability company],
- spol. s r.o. [lim. liab. comp.],
- s.r.o. [ltd.]

The registered capital of the limited liability company must be at least CZK 200,000. The capital contribution of each member must be at least CZK 20,000. If a member intends to provide a non-cash capital contribution to the registered capital, this contribution must be valued by an expert witness appointed by a court. If the company has a sole member, his capital contribution must be paid fully prior to the submission of the motion for the registration of the company in the Commercial Register. If the company has more members, then at least 30% of each cash capital contribution must be paid. The sum of all paid capital contributions prior to the submission of the motion for the registration of the limited liability company in the Commercial Register must be at least CZK 100,000. The extent of payment of members' non-cash capital contributions is also decisive for the extent of the members' liability. Members of a limited liability company are liable for the company's payables up to the sum of unpaid parts of capital contributions of all members according to the situation recorded in the Commercial Register. Therefore the actual extent of payment is not decisive. The situation recorded in the Commercial Register is relevant. In addition to the capital contribution obligation the General Meeting can decide to impose an "obligation to provide an extra payment" on the members. The member's extra payment in excess of his capital contribution cannot be greater than one half of the value of his capital contribution. It is important to draw the attention to the fact that the performance of this obligation to provide extra payment does not influence the amount of the member's capital contribution and his ownership interest.

Member's participation in the company is defined by his ownership interest. The law stipulates that an ownership interest is another property value. However, since all components of the ownership right can be exercised in the case of the ownership interest, i.e. it can be possessed, used, be subject to *usus fructus* and it can be disposed of, the case law deduced that it is the object of ownership and operates with it as with a thing, as appropriate. The member can transfer the ownership interest to another member or a third party. While the

Commercial Code does not require approval of the supreme body in case of transfer to a third party, when transferring the ownership interest to another member the approval of the General Meeting is necessary. The reason for this is that when transferring the ownership interest to another existing member, the proportion of votes among the members can significantly change. The ownership interest can be transferred in return for consideration or gratuitously. If the approval of the General Meeting is necessary for the transfer of the ownership interest, this approval is in the form of a notarial record. The agreement on the transfer of the ownership interest must be in writing with officially authenticated signatures of the transferor and transferee. In the agreement on the transfer of the ownership interest the transferee must also declare that he accedes to the Memorandum of Association of the limited liability company whose ownership interest he acquires. Subsequently the agreement in force is submitted to the Commercial Register, in which the information on the composition of members of the limited liability company is changed.

It is also possible to split the ownership interest in connection with its transfer or inheritance. However, when splitting the ownership interest it is necessary to bear in mind that the capital contribution connected with the ownership interest must be at least the amount of the minimum capital contribution, i.e. CZK 20,000. It also follows from the above that the ownership interest is the object of inheritance. However, the members can rule out the inheritance of the ownership interest in the Memorandum of Association. It can also happen that one ownership interest becomes a common property of several persons in consequence of inheritance. In this case an heir is entitled to a settlement share. As the ownership interest can be split, it can also be united again. This is because a member with limited liability can have only one ownership interest in a specific company. The ownership interest, as any other property value, can be object of enforcement of a decision or execution affecting the member's assets.

The ownership interest can also be subject to lien. The lien of the ownership interest is created upon the entry into the Commercial Register on the basis of a written agreement with officially authenticated signatures of the lienor and the lienee. In order to create the lien of an ownership interest the approval of the General Meeting is necessary in the same cases as when transferring the interest. The lien ceases to exist upon the entry into effect of its striking off from the Commercial Register upon a confirmation of it ceasing to exist. During the existence of the lien the member continues to exercise rights related to the ownership interest, but all considerations arising from the interest belong to the lienee. If those considerations are not sufficient to pay the receivable of the lienee, he can propose sale of the ownership interest subject to lien by an auction or in a public tendering process. The proceeds are used, first of all, to meet the costs of the sale and the receivable of the lienee and then the remainder is returned to the original owner of the interest. If the ownership interest subject to lien is not converted into money in any of the above ways, the lienee can agree with the lienor, i.e. the member, that the former would assume the ownership interest subject to lien to settle the receivable. The other members have no possibility to interfere with this change of a member. For that reason an amendment to the provisions is planned that would establish a pre-emption right of the other members regarding the ownership interest subject to lien. The lienee could assume the ownership interest only if the other members do not use the opportunity to acquire the ownership interest subject to lien in priority.

Since all the attributes of the ownership right can be exercised in respect of an ownership interest, the case law has also deduced already that the right to an ownership interest can be subject to adverse possession. When this right can be subject to adverse possession, the ownership interest can also be subject to possession. On the basis of the above the theory also deduced that the ownership interest could also be abandoned or expropriated with reference to the above arguments.

In addition to the common ways of termination of the member's participation in the limited liability company, which are the transfer of the ownership interest, death or dissolution of the member, dissolution of the limited liability company, execution or enforcement of a decision, the Commercial Code provides for other ways too. It is further possible to terminate the member's participation in the limited liability company by an agreement of all members, removal of the member by a decision of the General Meeting or a court decision and cancellation of the member's participation by a court decision. The Act on Transformation of Companies and Cooperatives provides for a special alternative, leaving the company which was mentioned in one of the preceding chapters. If the member's participation in the company is to be terminated on the basis of an agreement, all members of the limited liability company must give their consent to the agreement and the agreement must be in writing with officially authenticated signatures. If a member of the limited liability company believes that it would not be fair to require him to stay in the company and if it is not possible for the members to reach an agreement on the termination of his participation, he can request a court to cancel his participation in the company. For that purpose he must provide serious reasons that prove the unfairness of the requirement for his stay and also the seriousness of those reasons. The case law deduced that such reasons, for which the member cannot be fairly required to stay in the company, are, for example, serious health problems arising in relation to his participation in the company. Also the company itself has an opportunity to suggest termination of a member's participation in the company. The Commercial Code provides for the possibility of removing a member. A member can be removed from the company only if he seriously violates his obligations, if he was requested to remedy the situation and if he was advised in writing of the possibility of a sanction in the form of removal from the company. The company's General Meeting or a court can decide to remove a member from the limited liability company. The company's General Meeting can decide to remove a member from the company in two cases only. The first reason for the removal of the member by a decision of the General Meeting is the member's failure to perform his capital contribution obligation. The second reason is the member's failure to perform his obligation to provide extra payment. Both cases concern member's fundamental obligations of property nature and the failure to perform them can have serious consequences for the company. In addition to the fact that the satisfaction of the reason for the removal of the member by a decision of the General Meeting is easily provable, also the seriousness of both reasons is evident. In other cases of violations of member's obligations a court decides on the seriousness and satisfaction of other conditions for the removal of a member. In all cases of termination of member's participation in the limited liability company the member's ownership interest becomes "vacant" and passes to the disposal of the company. The company either transfers this vacant ownership interest to a new member, existing member, or it splits the ownership interest among the existing members, or it decreases the registered capital by the amount of the capital contribution of the removed member. However, in that case it is necessary to take into consideration that the amount of the registered capital cannot be decreased below the minimum level of CZK 200,000. The member, whose participation in the company ended, is entitled to a settlement share.

The organisation structure has at least two levels. The supreme body is the General Meeting composed of all members. The governing body of the limited liability company are Managing Directors. In the limited liability company also a Supervisory Board can be established, but this body is not mandatory for this company form. The General Meeting does not take place in the limited liability company only if the company has a sole member. In such case this member himself exercises the competences of the General Meeting.

The General Meeting is therefore the supreme body of the limited liability company. It is quorate with the presence of at least one half of all votes of the members and adopts decisions by a majority of votes of present members. The Commercial Code provides for a qualified majority of votes necessary for an adoption of a decision in case of serious issues within the competence of the General Meeting. The Code stipulates that each member has one vote for each CZK 1,000 of his capital contribution. The members can provide for a different number of votes of individual members in the Memorandum of Association. It is a rule that the member's ownership interest and number of votes is based on the ratios of members' capital contributions. However, the members can decide in the Memorandum of Association to specify all the above quantities in a different way. The General Meeting holds its meeting at least once a year and it is convened by the Managing Directors using a written invitation at least 15 days prior to the planned date of the General Meeting. Minutes of the General Meeting are recorded and the Managing Directors are responsible for that.

The competences of the General Meeting include, in particular:

- approval of acts made on behalf of the company prior to its incorporation,
- approval of annual, extraordinary and consolidated and in cases provided by law also interim financial

statements, decision on distribution of a profit or other own resources and on payment of a loss,
- adoption of Articles of Association and their amendments,
- decision on an amendment to the contents of the Memorandum of Association, if the contents are not amended on the basis of other legal facts,
- decision on increase or decrease of the registered capital or to allow non-cash capital contribution or on the possibility of setting off a cash receivable against the company with a receivable for the payment of the capital contribution,
- appointment, removal and remuneration of Managing Directors,
- appointment, removal and remuneration of members of the Supervisory Board,
- removal of a member,
- appointment, removal and remuneration of a liquidator and decision on the winding-up of the company with a liquidation, if the Memorandum of Association allows that,
- approval of agreements concerning transfer, lease or lien of an undertaking,
- decision on merger, transfer of assets to a member, division or change of the legal form,
- approval of a control agreement, agreement on the transfer of profit and agreement on a silent partnership and their amendments,
- approval of an agreement on the exercise of a function,
- approval of a provision of financial assistance,
- other issues included among the competences of the General Meeting on a statutory basis or in the Memorandum of Association,
- conferring and withdrawing a *procuration* [*"der prokurist"* within the meaning of German speaking countries' law] etc.

The members exercise their rights arising from the ownership interest particularly by exercising their voting right at General

Meetings. The member can participate in a General Meeting either in person or he can be represented. The member can exercise his voting right also after the end of the General Meeting, if he did not participate in it. In that case he uses his voting right so that within one month from the General Meeting he sends to the company his statement on the decision proposed at the General Meeting. This statement, if he votes in favour of the decision, must have the same form as required by law for the General Meeting decision. Therefore, if a General Meeting decision has to have the form of a notarial record, also the subsequent statement containing a vote in favour of the decision must have the form of a notarial record. In addition to the above methods, the members can also vote completely outside a General Meeting. In that case the Managing Director draws up a proposal for a General Meeting decision, sends it to the members and invites them to express their opinion on the proposed decision within a mentioned time limit. In that case a member's silence means disagreement with the proposed text of the decision. The principle of maintenance of the legal form required for a General Meeting decision and the member's statement applies in this case too. After the lapse of the time limit set in the notification the Managing Director informs the members of the outcome of their voting outside the General Meeting and carries out other formal procedures following the adopted decision.

The governing body is one or more Managing Directors. The General Meeting elects and removes the Managing Directors. A Managing Director does not have to be a member of the limited liability company. Unless provided for otherwise in the Memorandum of Association, each Managing Director acts on behalf of the company independently. The Managing Director is subject to a non-competition clause, which the Memorandum of Association can extend to the members as well. The Managing Directors, as a governing body, are also subject to the general requirements for the exercise of their function and a necessity of absence of an obstacle for the exercise of their function, as mentioned in the part containing the general reading. The quality of the Managing Directors' activities is assessed in light of the principle of due professional and fiduciary diligence. The fundamental obligations of the Managing Director are, in particular:

- to act on behalf of the company with third parties,
- to pursue his function with due professional and fiduciary diligence,
- to convene the General Meeting and to ensure minutes of its meeting,
- to ensure bookkeeping,
- to report and send statements to the General Meeting,
- to provide the members with information and requested documents for consultation and check,
- to keep the list of members etc.

The Supervisory Board is a voluntary body of the limited liability company. The same rules as in the case of the company's Managing Directors apply to the members of the Supervisory Board, their election and removal, quality of the exercise of their function etc. With regard to the competences of this body the company's Managing Director cannot be a member of the Supervisory Board. The Supervisory Board, if established, has at least three members which are subject to the non-competition clause too. The competences of the Supervisory Board, if established, include, in particular:

- supervision of the Managing Directors' activities,
- to consult the trade and accounting books and other documents and to check information contained therein,
- review of annual, extraordinary and consolidated, or also interim financial statements and a proposal for the distribution of a profit or payment of a loss and submission of its statement to the General Meeting,
- reporting to the General Meeting within a time limit set by the Memorandum of Association, otherwise annually,
- participation in the General Meetings,
- convening the General Meeting etc.

The members' rights and obligations can be divided into property and non-property ones. The member's fundamental property right is the right to a profit share, a share of a liquidation balance or to a settlement share. The fundamental property obligation is the capital contribution obligation. Other member's obligations include, in particular, the obligation to provide extra payment, if the

General Meeting decides on it, the obligation to respect the non-competition clause, if the Memorandum of Association provides for that, the obligation of loyalty etc. The fundamental non-property right is the participation in the General Meeting and exercise of the voting right at the General Meeting or outside of it. Other member's fundamental rights are right to information, under certain circumstances also the right to convene the General Meeting or to request the Managing Director to convene the General Meeting, the right to act on behalf of the company in extreme cases, the right to request the court to cancel his participation in the company, the right to bring an action against another member who is in default with the payment of his capital contribution, the right to bring an action against the Managing Director who is liable for damage in respect of the company etc.

As mentioned above, the registered capital of the limited liability company is composed of the sum of capital contributions of all members. Its minimum value is CZK 200,000 and the minimum capital contribution of each member must be CZK 20,000. These values have to be maintained even when changing the registered capital, which can be increased or decreased by a decision of the General Meeting. The registered capital can be increased by a cash capital contribution only after the existing cash capital contributions have been paid completely. The registered capital can be increased by a non-cash capital contribution without that limitation. The registered capital of the limited liability company can be increased in two ways. The first one is the assumption of an obligation to provide a new capital contribution. The existing members have a priority right to assume new capital contributions. They can assume a new capital contribution in the proportions of their existing ownership interests, in the proportions agreed or only one of the existing members can assume the capital contribution. The General Meeting decision to increase the registered capital must include:

- amount by which the registered capital is increased,
- time limit within which the obligations to increase the capital contribution or to assume a new capital contribution must be undertaken, or

- subject matter of the non-cash capital contribution and the amount that is counted as the member's capital contribution on the basis of an expert opinion.

Assumption of the obligation to make a new capital contribution must be done in writing and the signature must be officially authenticated. The person who assumes the new capital contribution must also declare in the declaration of the assumption of the capital contribution that he accedes to the Memorandum of Association. This way of increasing the registered capital is described as effective, because the company's financial situation actually improves. The second way, consisting in the increase of the registered capital from own resources, is described as nominal, because it actually concerns an accounting operation. The result of this accounting operation is the increase of the capital contribution of all members in the proportions of their existing capital contributions and this increase comes from the company's own resources shown in the financial statements.

The registered capital can be decreased by a capital contribution belonging to the ownership interest which is at the company's disposal. The registered capital can also be decreased by a proportionate decrease of the capital contributions of the existing members. Disproportionate decrease of the members' capital contributions can be used to decrease the registered capital only if the registered capital is decreased by a part of a member's capital contribution in respect of which the member is at default, or if all members agree with that. The General Meeting decision to decrease the registered capital includes:

- amount by which the registered capital is decreased,
- information on how the amounts of the members' capital contributions change,
- information on whether the amount corresponding to the decrease of the registered capital would be completely or partly paid to the members or whether the obligation to pay the capital contribution would be waived or information on another way of disposing with that amount.

Increase and decrease of the registered capital comes into effect only upon the registration of this change in the Commercial Register. Therefore the registration is of constitutive nature. Extended requirements of formal nature are imposed on the process of decrease of the registered capital because this fact can negatively influence the company's creditors. For that reason the Managing Directors are obligated to publish the decision on the decrease of the registered capital and the invitation for the creditors to submit their receivables twice in a row with certain time difference in the Commercial Journal. The limited liability company must then settle the receivables of the creditors who applied or it must provide these creditors with a reasonable security for their claims. The above is a condition for the registration of the decrease of the registered capital in the Commercial Register.

2.3.2 Public company limited by shares

Public company limited by shares is a clear form of stock corporation. Stockholders are not liable for company's liabilities, their personal concern in activities of the company is not expected and they have investments obligation. Stockholders provide investments in the public company limited by shares in forms of payments of so-called rate of issue of their subscribed shares. The rate of issue is formed by face value of a share, quoted on the share, and by so-called share premium, i.e. by the value paid over the face value of the share.

Public company limited by shares may be incorporated by a sole shareholder. Its incorporation requires to specify company's name, this name's addendum then forms one of the following descriptions that specify legal form:

- akciová společnost (public company limited by shares),
- akc. spol.
- a.s. (plc.)

As distinct from other forms of commercial companies, two deeds of incorporation are required to incorporate public company limited by shares: Memorandum of Association and Articles of Association. Both documents require a form of notarial deed, whereas during incorporation of a company the Articles of Association represent appendix to the Memorandum of Association and only consequently it becomes an original document, the importance of which exceeds The Memorandum of Association under public company's limited by shares existence. The Memorandum of Association must especially determine following obligatory content:

- company name, residence and subject of business (activity),
- proposed registered capital,
- number of shares and their face value, form of shares' issue, as well as specification if the shares are registered shares of bearer shares, eventually how many shares will be registered shares and how many will be bearer shares; whether different kinds of shares shall be issued, their name and description of rights connected to them, eventually information on restrictions on convertibility to registered shares,
- how many shares are subscribed by which shareholder, their rate of issue, way and deadline for redemption of the rate of issue, and specification of investment the rate of issue will be redeemed,
- whether the shares' rate of issue is redeemed from non-monetary investments, as well as specifying the subject of non-monatery investment and the way of its amortization, number, face value, form and type of shares that will be issued for this non-monatery investment,
- at least approximate amount of expences originating from the incorporation of the company,
- Investments administrator designation
- If at least a part of shares shall be issued in shares based on public offer, then also these information must be added:
- place and period of subscription of shares, which may not be shorter than two weeks,

- procedure of subscription of shares, especially whether efficiency of shares' subscription upon reaching or exceeding proposed registered capital amount will be judged from the date of shares' subscription, eventually whether it is possible to reduce the number of subscribed shares to individual subscribers, who will subscribe shares at the same time, based on the rate of face values of those shares that they have subscribed,
- whether incorporators admit subscription of shares that exceed proposed registered capital, procedure by such as subscription,
- stipulation that persons concerned may redeem share's rate of issue only from monatery investments,
- place, period, eventually bank or saving and credit cooperative account for the rate of issue's redemption,
- rate of issue of subscribing shares or a method of its definition; the rate of issue or the method of its definition must be the same for all subscribers, unless provided otherwise,
- way to convene general meeting and place of its proceedings,
- Draft of the Articles of Association.
- The Articles of Association must specify following obligatory requirements:
- Company name and residence of the company,
- Subject of business (activity),
- Amount of registered capital and mode of redemption of shares' rate of issue,
- Number of shares and their face value, form of shares' issue, as well as specification if the shares will be registered shares of bearer shares, eventually how many shares will be registered shares and how many will be bearer shares,
- Number of votes related to one share and method of voting in general meeting; if the company issued shares in different face value, number of votes that correspond to each of these different face values,

- Course of general meeting convening, its scope and way of its decision making,
- Definite number of members of management, supervisory board or other bodies, duration of body member's term of office, as well as specification of their scope and way of decision making, if these are incorporated,
- Course of setting up a surplus fund and level which company is liable to replenish, and way of replenishment,
- Course of profit division and loss covering,
- Consequencies of delinquency to pay subscribed shares on time,
- Rules of procedure of increasing and reducing registered capital, especially possibility to reduce registered capital by withdrawing the shares in a ballot from circulation,
- Procedure of completing and modifying the articles of association,
- Other data, unless provided otherwise.

The comparison of contentual requirements has itself brought number of doubts on the sense of double deeds of incorporation and there are some proposals to use only one of them.

It is possible to incorporate a public company limited by shares in two ways. The first way is incorporation based on shares public offering; the other way is incorporation without shares public offering. Registered capital of a public company limited by shares is given by the sum of face values of all shares of the public company limited by shares, whereas a share represents shareholder's proportional share of the company. In case of the incorporation of a public company limited by shares with shares public offering, the registered capital must amount at least CZK 20,000,000; in case of the incorporation of a public company limited by shares without shares public offering, the registered capital must amount at least CZK 2,000,000.

The determinant by the incorporation of a public company limited by shares with shares public offering is the number of subscribed shares. After setting up the public offering, persons interested to subscribe shares are expected, with necessity to reach at least CZK 20,000,000 in the sum of subscribed shares' face values. If sufficient number of interested persons to subscribe shares is not found, the rest of unsubscribed shares may be subscribed by incorporators themselves. Persons interested in subscription are registered in a deed of subscribers. As soon as the sufficient number of shares is subscribed in the way the sum of their face value reaches the level of required registered capital, the incorporators may decide to reject subsription of other shares. Thereby the subscribed shares shall correspond to the registered capital exactly anticipated in the deed of incorporation. The incorporators may also concede the subscription of shares over the anticipated capital and reach that way registered capital higher than intented. After termination of the subscription, registered capital amount is consequently decided on subscribed shares amount. If the minimal requested registered capital amount is not reached by shares' subscription, the incorporators may decide to subscribe the missing amount themselves, or the whole subscriptions is inoperative and the public company limited by shares shall not be formed. If sufficient number of shares has been subscribed, and at least 30% of all shares' face value and contingent share premium has been redeemed, the incorporators convene constituent general meeting. The task of the constituent general meeting is to:

- Decide about incorporation of a company,
- Approve its Articles of association,
- Elect company's bodies, which general meeting is entitled to elect by contract,
- State company name,
- Decide about its registered capital if the shares have been subscribed over anticipated registered capital amount, and others.

The course of constituent general meeting' process is recorded in a form of notarial deed. Another notarial deed is drawn up of the decision the Articles of association were approved, whereas agreed text of the Articles of association is enclosed to the notarial record.

If public company limited by shares is incorporated without shares public offering, incorporators subscribe respectively all shares needed to reach stated registered capital amount and they also discharge all constituent general meeting's functions.

Public company limited by shares is formed, as in case of other commercial companies, only after its registration into the Companies Register. Application to the Companies Register is signed by all members of board of directors and all appendices requested by legal regulations are enclosed to the application.

Public company limited by shares may issue several types of commercial papers. The basic commercial papers are shares; others are interim certificates, time warrants, stock warrants, priority and exchangeable bonds. The shares represent shareholders' proportional share of the company. They may be issued in book or documentary form, registered shares of bearer shares. If company issued documentary registered shares, the public company limited by shares or a person responsible for booked shares recording keeps shareholders register. Until a shareholder does not completely redeem face value and contingent share premium, share cannot be issued. For the period of complete redemption of above mentioned values, company gives him over an interim certificate that states especially number of subscribed shares, their basic characteristics and redempiton range. Stock warrant has a similar relevance. It is issued in connection with registered capital increased through new shares. Even in case that a shareholder has completely redeemed shares subscribed by him, the shares cannot be issued before the increasement of registered capital is registred into the Companies Register. As the registered capital is composed by sum of all issued shares' face value, the shares cannot be issued before the new increased registered capital amount is registered into the Companies Register. For this transitory period, a future shareholder is given a stock warrant. As it is possible to separate preferential subscription of shares from the shares, and preference and exchangeable rights from the bonds, so-called window warrants, that are connected to above mentioned separated rights, are issued. Public company limited by shares may issue exchangeable and priority bonds only in case that their issue is admited in articles of associations and that the company obtained necessary permissions for bonds' issue. Exchangeable bonds contain not only the right to redeem their face value and relevant profit, but also the right to exchange them for shares. Priority bonds contain the right of preferential subscription of shares. They obtain the meaning especially in relation to conditional registered capital increasement.

Shares specify shareholders' rights and obligations. Basic obligations are primarly shares' rate of issue redemption, obligation to present interim certificates to be changed for shares, eventually to present shares when registered capital is reduce by withdrawing the shares in a ballot from circulation, duty to bid an offer to buy other subscriber's bond back in cases prescribed by law, and in cases prescribed by law also notification duty. One of the shareholder's basic rights is especially right of profit share, share in liquidation balance, settling in case of purchase of shares or their withdrawal, right to exercise the voting right in general meeting, preferential right to subscribe new shares, right to seek shares purchased by company, or right to offer to repurchase a share in cases prescribed by the law. Except above mentioned basic rights, the Commercial Code describes so-called minority group of shareholders. This group consists of shareholders whose face value is, based on registered capital amount, 5% of capital total amount, and if a public company limited by shares has less than CZK 100,000,000 it suffices to reach the border of 3% of capital total amount. Public limited company's minority has following rights:

- to ask board of directors to include an item of their concern in general meeting agenda; if the request was received after sending general meeting invitation or after publishing its proceedings, the board of directors publishes completion of the general meeting agenda within ten days before the general meeting is held, if appointed, before record date for the general meeting participation as provided by law and by the articles of association for general meeting convocation,
- to ask supervisory board a review of board of directors' activity execution in matters appointed by the request,
- to ask supervisory board to claim damages from a board of directors member in favour of the company,
- to entrust board of directors with bringing an action for shares' rate of issue redemption against shareholders

that are in delay with its redemption, or with declaring shares invalidity,

- to claim damages independently or shares' rate of issue redemption on behalf of the company if neither board of directors or supervisory board has granted their action,
- to appoint an expert to review a report about relations between controlled person and connected persons, if there are serious reasons for that, and others.

Public company's limited by shares organisational structure represents dual model of commercial company management. Beside the supreme body, there are two other strong bodies, that is a board of directors as governing body and a supervisory board. Both bodies are generally independant on each other. However, the Commercial Code allows to strengthen the supervisory board so the articles of association state that members of the board of directors are elected and suspended by the supervisory board.

The general meeting is the supreme body of a public company limited by shares. It consists of company's shareholders. The general meeting is held at least once per year. The general meeting is convened by the board of directors, by its particular member, in case of need by the supervisory board and in extreme case by the public company's minority. The last one consists of the shareholders whose all shares' face value sum corresponds to at least 3%, event. 5%, in case of companies with registered capital higher than CZK 100,000,000 of total registered capital. The general meeting is convened by written invitation in case that the company issued registered shares, or by written announcement published in the Commercial bulletin and in one statewide distributed press, this press is appointed in company's articles of association. The invitation or the announcement contain at least:

- Company name and company's residence,
- Place, date and hour of the general meeting proceedings,
- Indication if the convened general meeting is ordinary, extraordinary or substitutional,
- General meeting agenda,

- Record date for participation on the general meeting, if appointed, and explanation of its relevance in the general meeting's election.

The general meeting is quorate only if shareholders, whose shares represent at least 30% of registered capital, are present. The general meeting decides common matters by simple majority of present shareholders. For more important decisions of the general meeting, the Commercial Code defines stricter qualified majorities of votes needed to make a decision. The scope of the general meeting includes especially:

- making decision on the articles of associations changes, if the change is not the consequence of the registered capital increased by the board of directors, or if the change is the consequence of other legal facts,
- making decision on increasing or reducing the registered capital or on the board of directors delegation or on the possibility to include financial debt toward the company against rate of issue redemption debt,
- making decision on reducing the registered capital and on bonds' issue,
- election and suspension of a member of boards of directors, if the articles of association does not appoint that members are elected and suspended by supervisory board,
- election and voting off members of supervisory board and members of other bodies appointed by the articles of association, except for elected and voted off members of supervisory board,
- ordinary or extraordinary final accounts authorisation and consolidated final accounts and in cases prescribed by law also interlocutory final accounts authorisation, decision on profit or other proper assets division, or on director's fees regulation or decision on covering a loss,
- making decision on members of board of directors' and supervisory board's remuneration,

- making decision on quotation of company's subscriber commercial papers under special legal regulations, and on their withdrawal from trading on Czech or foreign trade,
- making decision on winding-up the company with liquidation, nomination and removal of a liquidator, incl. stating of his remuneration, proposal of liquidation surplus allotment approval,
- making decision on fusion, on assets transfer to one shareholder, or on division, event. legal form of transformation,
- Deeds of sale, lease or suspension of a company or its part approval,
- actions done on behalf of the company before the company formation approval,
- control deed, deed of profit transfer and of silent partnership and their modifications, and others approval.

General meeting proceedings are recorded; recording provided by a board of directors and submited within 30 days from general meeting proceedings. Besides others, the minutes include especially description of agenda discussion and of voting results. If the company has a sole shareholder, the general meeting is not held and the sole shareholder himself discharges its scope.

Governing body of public company limited by shares is a board of directors. The board of directors has at least three members, except for unipersonal company where the sole shareholder fully determines the number of the body members. The board of directors members' period of office is appointed by articles of association and may be no longer than 5 years. The board of directors members should meet general requirements to discharge of the office of a commercial company's body member, there mustn't be any obstacles to discharge his office, the person must discharge his activities duly, meets requirements to ban on competitive conduct and incompability with supervisory board member' office. The main targets of board of directors are especially:

- Acting towards third persons and company's commercial management,
- Securing regular accounting procedures conducting, incl. final accounts,
- Securing execution of general meeting's minutes,
- Supplying shareholders with requested information and providing requested documents for control,
- Issuing proposal of company's profit share allotment, eventually its loss cover,
- General meeting convocation,
- Issuing business activities reports and company's assets state report, and submitting them to general meeting,
- Deciding company's registered capital increasement by subsribing new shares or from proper assets if authorised by general meeting,
- Discharging whole scope not prescribed by law or by articles of association for general meeting or for supervisory board.

Minutes are taken also from board of directors' proceedings, including especially description of agenda, discussion of its particular points and voting. Proceedings' minutes may be an important basis for individual members' discharge of office, i.e. to qualify if they acted duly.

Public company's limited by shares control body is a supervisory board. It has at least three members and in case of higher number of members, their number must be dividable by three. Its reason is employees' interests protection. That is, if number of company's employess reaches over 50, they have the right to vote at least 1/3 of supervisory board members, however not more than ½ of members. Supervisory board members elected by employees have one substantial advantage against other members. Minutes are taken also from supervisory board proceedings. While other members of this body must request to state their diverse opinion in the minutes, the diverse opinion of supervisory board members is stated in the minutes automatically. From view of requirements to discharge of office, its quality, incompability of its discharge, period of office etc., there are the same requirements as for company's board of directors. The scope of supervisory board is especially:

- to convene general meeting if requested by company's interests,
- to supervise board of directors' discharge of activity and company's business activity practice,
- to consult company's documents and records and to control all data contained in these documents and records,
- to review final accounts,
- to review proposal of company's profit share and loss allotment,
- to appoint and vote off board of directors members if authorised by deed of incorporation,
- to take part in company's general meeting proceedings,
- to inform general meeting about control activity results,
- to approve chosen decisions of the board of directors,
- to act on behalf of the company against a board of director's member resposible for damages occured in relation with his action to the company, and others.
- As above mentioned, public company limited by shares registered capital should reach at least CZK 2,000,000, or CZK 20,000,000, depending on the way of company's incorporation. Registered capital is given by the sum of all subscribed shares' face value. Changes of the registered capital are decided entirely by general meeting that may, however, authorise the registered capital increasing from proper assets or from subscription of new shares on board of directors. This authorisation is consequently entered in Companies Register's Collection of documents. If general meeting shall decide upon registered capital increasement, this information must be included in invitation or announcement of the general meeting proceedings, as well as basic information on limits, reasons and methods of registered capital change. The registered

capital change is decided by qualified majority of all votes. The registered capital changes may be effective, leading to real changes in capital's property situation, and nominal, representing basically a type of an account change.

The registered capital may be increased by following:

- Increasing subscription of new shares, i.e. by distribution of new shares among current shareholders with pre-emption right, or by sistributing them among other potential buyers.
- Increasing from proper assets, i.e. by increasing face value of hitherto subscribed shares.
- Increasement conditioned by subscription rate of priority and exchangeable bonds with consequent rate of rights utilisation arising from them.
- Combined way, which in case of declination of quoted shares rate combines registered capital increasing from new shares subscription and registered capital increasement from proper resources.

Intention to reduce the registered capital must be published especially because of creditors' protection. Creditors must be also informed about intention to reduce the registered capital and if required, they must be provided with security of their payable accounts, or these payable accounts must be settled. Settlement or security of accounts payable must be consequently proved at a court, which shall register registered capital reduction in Companies Register. Registered capital is reduced only at the moment of its registration in Companies Register. Also in this case, the entry is of constitutive character. The registered capital may be reduced by following:

- Reducing shares' and interim certificates' face value proportionally at all shares, eventually by unpaid part of some shares' rate of issue.
- Shares withdrawal from circulation based on ballot with payment of compensation to those shareholders who hereby lose their shares.

- Shares withdrawal based on a proposal, also in this case with compensation provided to those shareholders who accept company's offer.
- Abandoning shares issuing within the extent of shareholders delay with shares face value redemption.

Except for registered capital, public company limited by shares sets up also a surplus fund usable for company's loss cover. The surplus fund is set up to at least 20% of registered capital amount.

Public company limited by shares is, as well as all commercial companies, wound-up by an authorised body and dissolved by its erasure from the Companies Register. Public company limited by shares may be wound-up with liquidation or without liquidation with a successor in title.

2.3.3 COMMERCIAL COMPANIES AS OBJECTS OF SPECIAL LEGAL REGULATIONS

Except for above mentioned forms of commercial companies, there is a number of other particular legal regulations that regulate also other forms of business legal entities. These are especially insurance companies, investment companies and investment funds, Stock exchange, Commodity exchange, pension funds, banks and saving banks, and state business. State business has a special position as its legal regulation, object of special legal regulation, is relatively compact, as its incorporator may be only the state, and as it is a really specific legal entity. Other forms of mentioned business legal entities are also objects of special legal regulations, they have their particularities in organizational structure etc., and they have one fundamental common feature. The basis of their legal regulation is the Commercial Code, through reference regulation of most frequently public company's limited by shares legal regulation. Special legal regulations thus regulate especially variances of common legal regulation of commercial company's sample type stated by the Commercial Code. The really common feature of all above mentioned business legal entities, that are object of special legal regulations, is the fact that they are registered in the Companies Register, and as such, from the view of Czech commercial law, they are considered businesses, regardless of their actual activity.

2.4 COOPERATIVES

Although a cooperative is a juristic person, corporation, business with regard to its obligatory registration in the Commercial Register, it is not a company. However, since a number of characteristics and concepts of cooperatives is similar to companies, provisions on the cooperatives in the Commercial Code immediately follow the ones on the public company limited by shares. The provisions are designed so that general definitions and concepts of companies apply to the cooperatives as well. The part of the Commercial Code dedicated to cooperatives therefore governs, in particular, special issues different from the general provisions on companies. The purpose of the cooperative is to conduct business or to secure economic, social, cultural, housing or other needs of the cooperative's members. The cooperative must have at least two members if these are juristic persons, otherwise it must have at least five members. Members of the cooperative are not liable for its payables. The cooperative is liable for its payables with its total assets.

The cooperative creates "registered capital" amounting to at least CZK 50,000. Each member is obligated to make a "basic member's contribution" in the amount provided for by the cooperative's Articles of Association. The members can undertake to pay "additional member's contribution" in addition to the basic member's contribution. If the members provide non-cash contributions, they do not have to be valued by an expert witness, unless it is required by the cooperative's Articles of Association. The non-cash contributions are valued exclusively in the way determined in the cooperative's Articles of Association. The cooperative is obligated to create an indivisible fund whose purpose is similar to the one of company's reserve fund. The indivisible fund has to be at least one half of the registered capital. The registered capital is the sum of member's contributions which the members undertook.

When forming a cooperative it is necessary to determine its name. The name has to have an end containing the specification that it is a cooperative. A founding Members Meeting is necessary for the formation of the cooperative. All interested persons who filed their application are present at this meeting. If the applicant does not agree with the text of the founding documents in the form in which they were adopted, immediately after the vote he can withdraw his application and he does not become a member of the cooperative. The founding Members Meeting has the following tasks:

- to determine the registered capital,
- to adopt the cooperative's Articles of Association,
- to elect members of the Board of Directors and the Control Commission.

The minutes of the founding Members Meeting are recorded in the form of a notarial record. The list of members together with their member's contributions is enclosed with this record. The Articles of Association are also drawn up in the form of a notarial record. It follows from the above that the Articles of Association are the cooperative's founding document. The mandatory essentials of the Articles are the following, in particular:

- name and registered office of the cooperative,
- area of business (activity),
- formation and termination of membership, rights and obligations of the members in relation to the cooperative and of the cooperative in relation to the members,
- amount of the basic member's contribution, and, if applicable, also the amount of entry contribution, the way of payment of member's contributions and settlement of a membership interest upon the termination of membership,
- cooperative's bodies and number of their members, their term of office, way of their establishment, competences and way how to convene them and way of their meetings,
- way of using the profit and payment of a possible loss,
- establishment and use of the indivisible fund, etc.

Similarly as companies, the cooperative is incorporated upon its registration in the Commercial Register on the basis of a motion signed by the members of the Board of Directors. In particular, the counterpart of the notarial record of the minutes of the founding meeting of the cooperative and the counterpart of the notarial record of the decision of the founding meeting of the cooperative on the adoption of the Articles of Association, the cooperative's Articles of Association and a document showing the payment of the set part of the registered capital are to be attached to that motion.

The cooperative keeps the list of its members. The membership of the cooperative is established in the following ways, in particular:

- at the formation of the cooperative on the day of the cooperative's incorporation,
- during the existence of the cooperative by an admission of a member on the basis of a written member application,
- transfer of membership, or
- in another way provided for in law (e.g. by inheritance).

The transfer of rights and obligations must be approved by the Board of Directors and such transfer is only possible if it is not ruled out by the Articles of Association. In case of cooperatives whose purpose is to satisfy the housing needs of its members the membership interest is always transferable and no approval of the cooperative's bodies is necessary. The membership rights are transferable by a written agreement. The transfer of the membership rights must be proven to the cooperative, or the transferor must inform about the transfer. In addition to the general ways of termination of membership, such as a transfer or a member's death, the membership also ends in consequence of a written agreement, leaving, removal, enforcement of a decision or in consequence of enforcement, insolvency or bankruptcy proceedings. When a member leaves the cooperative, he is obligated to provide reasons in the written notification. His membership ends after six months, at the latest, from the service of the document on the cooperative. A member of the cooperative can be removed by a decision of the Board of Directors. In case of an appeal filed by the removed member against that decision the Members Meeting, or a court in the last resort, upholds the decision. When the membership ends the member has a right to a settlement share, with the exception of the case of transfer.

The fundamental rights of the member of the cooperative include, in particular, the right to a profit share, the right to a satisfaction of needs for which the cooperative was formed, the right to participate in the management of the cooperative by exercising the voting rights, the right to transfer the membership interest, the right to leave the cooperative, the right to file an appeal against a decision of the Board of Directors on the removal from the cooperative to the Members Meeting or a court, the right to a settlement share and a share of a liquidation balance, the right to be elected into the cooperative's bodies, the right to file a motion with a court for the declaration of nullity of the Members Meeting, the right to resign from the function of an elected member of the cooperative's body etc. The fundamental obligation of the member of the cooperative is the payment of the member's contribution with a possible default interest.

The organisation structure depends on the size of the cooperative. If the cooperative has less than 50 members, the Members Meeting can also exercise the competences of the Board of Directors and the Control Commission. In that case the elected President is the governing body. In other cases the organisation structure of the cooperative corresponds to the dual model. The supreme body of the cooperative is its Members Meeting. This meeting can take place as a General Meeting of companies, or, if the number of members is large, as a partial meeting of elected delegates. The minutes of the Members Meeting are recorded in a similar way as in the case of General Meetings of companies. The Members Meeting takes place at least once a year and its competences includes, in particular:

- amendment of the Articles of Association,
- election and removal of members of the Board of Directors and the Control Commission,
- approval of annual financial statements,
- decision on the distribution and use of a profit, or the way of payment of a loss,

- decision on the increase or decrease of the registered capital,
- decision on fundamental issues of the concepts of the cooperative's development,
- decision on the winding-up of the cooperative with a liquidation or on the transformation of the cooperative,
- decision on the entry into agreements under Section 67a or on other significant property disposals,
- decision on the sale or other property disposals concerning immovables, in which there are flats, or concerning flats; the Members Meeting can adopt such decision only after a prior written consent of the majority of the members of the housing cooperative, who are tenants in the immovable concerned by the decision; this does not apply if the cooperative has an obligation to transfer a flat or non-residential premises to the ownership of the member who is the tenant.

The Board of Directors is the cooperative's governing body. In particular, the Board of Directors manages the cooperative's activities, decides on all issues not entrusted to the Members Meeting, acts on behalf of the cooperative in relation to third parties, fulfils the Members Meeting's decisions, ensures the bookkeeping etc.

The Control Commission is the cooperative's control body. Its main tasks include, in particular, the control of all the cooperative's activities, hearing complaints of the cooperative's members, it expresses its opinion on the financial statements and on the proposals for the distribution of a profit or payment of a loss, etc. From the point of view of non-competition, the term of office, creation and termination of the function, conditions for the exercise of the function, quality of the exercise of the function etc. the provisions governing the Board of Directors of a public company limited by shares apply *mutatis mutandis* to the cooperative's Board of Directors and Control Commission.

3. COMMERCIAL OBLIGATIONS

3.1 GENERAL REGULATION OF COMMERCIAL OBLIGATIONS

3.1.1 SUBJECT MATTER

The Czech valid legal regulation of a private obligation is included primarily in two fundamental codexes, in the Civil Code and in the Commercial Code. Since these two legal acts demonstrate a myriad of differences (protection of parties vs. autonomy of their will, acquisition of ownership from a (non)owner, the subjective vs. objective responsibility, the statute of limitations of three- vs. four years, the *ex tunc* vs. *ex nunc* effect of the withdrawal from a contract, the court competency, etc.), it is necessary to clearly determine the commercial obligations to which pertains the Commercial Code as *lex specialis* and to which applies the Civil Code only in a subsidiary manner. Specifically, there are absolute businesses subjected to the Commercial Code under any and all circumstances, the so called relative businesses whose subjection to the Commercial Code depends upon the nature of their participants and their subject matter, the so called facultative or election business and the so called accessory businesses:

To the group of the absolute commercial obligations belong namely:

- relations between the founders, members and statutory representatives of commercial companies and co-operatives and
- relations from merely commercial contracts (a lease and sale contract of an enterprise, a collateral right to a business share, a silent partnership contract, bank contracts – contracts on securities, credit contracts, contract on a letter of credit, collection contracts, a

bank deposit contract, a contract on a checking account, a contract on a deposit account, etc.).

To the group of relative commercial obligations belong especially:

- relations between entrepreneurs related to their entrepreneurial acitivity provided the entrepreneurship represents a continuous activity in its own name and on its´ own responsibility and in order to attain a profit and
- relations between the state, state organizations or independent local entities and entrepreneurs during their entrepreneurial activity if it relates to providing for public needs.

To the group of non mandatory (facultative) or election businesses belong relations about which parties have agreed, in writing, to submit them under the Commercial Code. If such an agreement aims to worsen the legal position of the contractual party which is not an entrepreneur, then such an agreement is invalid. In no case are the parties allowed to avoid the exclusive scope of application of the Civil Code for contracts which are regulated as type contracts by the Civil Code and (in the rest) possibly by the Commercial Code (e.g., rent or lend).

To the group of secondary (accessorial) businesses belong relations created for securing the above mentioned relations, i.e. the legal regime of the surety of absolute, relative or facultative businesses follows the legal regime of the secured relation and it is irrelevant whether the provider of the surety is an entrepreneur or not, or whether the matter is related to his entrepreneurship.

Aside from those four groups of obligations relations subjected to the Commercial Code, there are the so called absolute non businesses, i.e. relations expressly excluded from the regime of the Commercial Code. An example of this phenomena is the contract of insurance always subjected to the Civil Code.

Although the Commercial Code acknowledges the contractual freedom of the contractual parties, it includes three types of provisions from those it is not allowed to deflect. Those mandatory provisions are:

- basic provisions for type contracts according to the Commercial Code (see Chapter 3.2.);
- provisions which are expressly declared as mandatory by the Commercial Code (e.g., concerning the consideration of business practice while interpreting, or about declining to provide a legal protection to the enforcement of a right which is in contradiction to the principles of the honest business conduct, or about the exclusion of the possibility to rescind a contract concluded in distress under ostensibly unfavoreable conditions) and
- provisions ordering a written form for the legal act.

While determing rights and duties from the commercial obligation, the commercial custom practice, i.e. no written rules of behavior generally respected in the particular commercial branch, is respected, provided they do not contradict with the content of the contract or of the law.

Both the Civil Code and the Commercial Code set certain ethical limits. According to the Civil Code, the execution of rights and duties implied from civil obligations cannot, without legal justification, breach the rights and legitimate interests of others, and cannot be in contradiction with good manners. The Commercial code tends, instead of the concept of good manners, to the concept of honesty, and provides that the execution of rights in contradiction with principles of honest commerce does not enjoy any legal protection.

3.1.2 LEGAL ACTS

The requirements of a legal act are set generally by the Civil Code. Therefore, even a legal act creating a commercial obligation must be done under the sanction of invalidity:

- freely,
- seriously,
- specifically, and
- understandably.

A legal act can be done neither under the threat of violence, nor as a joke, nor unclearly nor in a manner that cannot be understood. Further, a legal act is invalid if its performance is from the beginning impossible, not realizable, or in breach of the law.

Naturally, any legal act must be expressed by a person competent to do so.

The Commercial code introduces a subjective point of view to determine if the invalidity is absolute or relative. If the invalidity of the legal act is laid down to protect only one party, then only such a party can invoke such invalidity.

The expression of will is interpreted by the intention of the acting person, provided such an intention either was known or must be known to the person to whom the act was addressed or such intention would be expected by a person in a similar position as the person to whom the act was addressed. The expressions used in commerce are interpreted according to the meaning which they generally have in commerce.

The interpretation is done while considering all related circumstances, including the negation about the conclusion of the contract, established practices of the parties and the following behavior of the parties. The doubts while interpreting a debatable expression of the will weighted upon the party which used such an expression as the first one.

The principle of the legal certainty in commercial relations outweighs to some extent the principal of the equality of the parties and their protection, i.e. the parties carry the business risk and cannot avoid the consequences of their behavior conducted in a commercially complicated situation which lead them into an economically unfavorable position. Therefore, the regulation of the Civil Code about the possibility of the rescission of a party which concluded the contract in distress under ostensibly unfavorable conditions will not apply to the relations regulated by the Commercial Code.

The principle of severity is applicable to contractual relations regulated by the Commercial Code, i.e. a conflict of law clause or an arbitration included in an invalid contract are invalid only if the cause of invalidity attains them. Similarly, the invalidity of such clauses does not affect the validity of the remaining part of the contract.

3.1.3 CONTRACT CONCLUSION

Negotiation and information provided before the conclusion of the contract can be legally protected. Concretely, if one party designates provided information as confidential, another party is bound by it and must not disclose it to third persons or use it for its own need in contradiction to its purpose. This duty of confidentiality is valid regardless of the conclusion or the lack of the conclusion of the contract. The breach of this duty generates the responsibility for the caused damage.

Contractual parties may conclude either a "type" contract, i.e. a contract expressly regulated by the Commercial Code, or a so called *innominate* (unnamed) contract, provided such a contract is enough specific. Blank forms used in business can be used for the conclusion of a contract. In addition, a part of a contract can be determined by a reference to general commercial terms, which are either known to the contracting parties or enclosed in the contract. If, in spite of this, the contract is not concluded and done from the beginning in a complete wording, it does not imply per se the invalidity, because the contractual parties can agree that a part of a contract will be completed later in an objective manner. Based on a written agreement, a missing part of a contract can be set by a court or by an agreed person.

A contract can be concluded orally, except in cases where the written form is prescribed by the Commercial Code or when one of the contractual parties expresses during the negotiation about the conclusion of the contract its will that the contract be concluded in a written form. Even an implied conclusion of a contract is not excluded. Taking into consideration the content of the offer to conclude a contract or based on past practices entered into by the parties, an addressee of the offer can express his acceptance by performing an act (e.g., sending the merchandise or paying the price) without informing the offeror about it. In such a case, the acceptance of the offer becomes effective in the moment of the performance of the act, provided it happens before the expiration of the decisive term for the acceptance of the offer.

The offer of the contract can be addressed to a concrete person or to an undetermined person or persons (a so called public offer). The expression of the will not meeting the specification requirements for a contractual offer is deemed to be a mere suggestion, a call for presenting offers to conclude a contract (e.g., the public tender).

A public offer can be revoked if the offeror informs about the revocation of the public offer before its acceptance in a manner in which the offer was published. Based on a public offer, a contract is concluded with a person which in compliance with the content of the public offer and in the term by its prescribed, otherwise in an appropriate term, first informs the offeror about its acceptance and subsequently the offeror confirms the conclusion of the contract. If a public offer is accepted simultaneously by several people, the offeror can choose to whom of these recepients he will confirm the conclusion of the contract. The offeror has to inform the recipient about the conclusion of the contract without any unnecessary delay after obtaining of the acceptance of the offer.

The contract for a future contract is covered by a particular regime. The contractual party or the contractual parties commit themselves by such a contract to conclude in a determined period a future contract with a subject matter performance which is determined at least in a general manner. If the obligated party later refuses to conclude the future contract, then the beneficiary party has a choice either to enforce the determination of the contract by the court or by an agreed upon person or sue for damages caused by the breach of the obligation to conclude the contract. Contrariwise, if the beneficiary party does not call the obligated party to conclude the future contract in the determined period, then the duty to conclude the future contract expires.

3.1.4 JOINT OBLIGATIONS

The establishment of the presumption of joint and several liability constitutes traditionally a part of the commercial regulation. If more debtors are obliged to the same performance, in doubts it is assumed that they are obliged jointly and severally. The creditor can ask for the performance from whichever among the debtors and at the same time the creditor is obliged to accept the performance from whichever debtor. If contrariwise it can be implied from the contract, or from the nature of the obligation, that debtors are not obliged to the same performance jointly and severally, then each co-debtor is bound only to the extent of its share in the obligation. In doubts, it is presumed that the co-debtors are bound by an equal share.

If regarding a not separable performance, a debtor is bound simultaneously toward more creditors, the debtor can request the performance from whichever of his debtors, unless the law or the contract do not state otherwise. Similarly, if more guarantors provide a guarantee for one single obligation, then each of them guarantees the entire obligation. The guarantor has the same rights toward others guarantors like co-debtors.

3.1.5 SECURING AN OBLIGATION

Taking into account the global economic crisis as well as particular circumstances, securing an obligation becomes often an indispensable part of the commercial obligation. A myriad of securing instruments exist.

Some of them have only the securing function (e.g., the guarantee), while others serve several functions, including the covering function (e.g., a bill of credit). Securing instruments are regulated across the

Czech Law and the Commercial Code sets only some of them, and in addition not in the full extent. The subsidiarity of the Civil Code is in this area not to be omitted.

To securing instruments expressly regulated by the Commercial Code belong the following:

- contractual penalty;
- suretyship;
- bank guarantee;
- acknowledgment of an obligation and
- financial security.

The contractual penalty is a written agreed on sanction for the breach of a contractual duty and it does not apply to the withdrawal from the contract. It must be agreed upon either it´s amount or the manner of the calculation of it´s amount. The regulation of the contractual penalty in the Commercial Code is not complete, and therefore appropriate provisions of the Civil Code are subsidiarily applied for the regime of the contractual penalty. In other words, the regime of a commercial contractual penalty illustrates the differences between the regulation according to the Civil Code and according to the Commercial Code when all provisions from the Commercial Code and some from the Civil Code are applied. The subjective attitude of the Civil Law allows the debtor to prove that he did not cause the breach and consequently excludes the rise of the creditor´s claim on the contractual penalty. Contrariwise, the objective attitude of the Commercial Code preserves the duty to pay the contractual penalty even if the debtor could satisfy his primary duty because of an unforseeable and unavoidable obstacle which has occurred independently of his will. However, these concepts are set as not mandatory and therefore the parties are allowed to divert from them. The obvious severity of the application of the contractual penalty under the Commercial Code is softened by the provision about the moderation right. Therefore a disproportionally high contractual penalty can be reduced by a court while considering the value and the importance of the secured duty, and this up to the amount of the damage arisen until the moment of the court decision about the breach of the contractual duty covered by this contractual penalty. On the contrary, the courts do not have the moderation right in respect to the civil obligations and can only either confirm the entire contractual penalty or pronounce the entire contractual penalty as disproportionate and so do not acknowledge even a part of it.

The suretyship is a written obligation of a third person, the guarantor, toward the creditor, that he will fulfill a specific valid obligation or it's part if the primary debtor does not do so. The creation of the suretyship is not hindered if the debtor's obligation is invalid due to the incompetency of the debtor to commit himself to obligations, and the guarantor was aware of this at the time of his declaration of the surety. The suretyship can cover a current obligation as well as a future obligation or an obligation which creation depends upon the satisfaction of a condition. Upon a request, the creditor must without any unnecessary delay inform the guarantor about the amount of the secured receivable and is allowed to claim the satisfaction of the obligation from the guarantor only if the debtor did not fulfill his due obligation in an appropriate time after a written request from the creditor.

The guarantor can assert toward the creditor all objections to which assertation is allowed the debtor and credit the debtor's receivables against the creditor, provided such a count towards would be allowed to the debtor in the case of the enforcement of the creditor's receivable against him. After the fulfillment of the primary obligation, for which the guarantor provides the suretyship, he obtains all rights of the creditor against the debtor and is allowed to ask for all documents and instruments, which has the creditor, and which are needed in order to enforce the primary claim against the primary debtor. The suretyship obligation follows the destiny of the secured primary obligation and expires at the moment of the expiration of the secured obligation, except in the case of the termination of the primary obligation due to the impossibility of the performance only on the side of the debtor or after the termination of the debtor who is a legal person. Similarly, due to the cession of the secured receivable, the rights from the suretyship passes on to the cessionary at the moment when the gauarantor is informed about the cession by the cessor or proven by the cessionary. The creditor's right toward the guarantor does not become statute-barred before the right toward the primary debtor becomes statute-barred.

The bank guarantee represents a particular suretyship and the provisions about the suretyship from the Commercial Code apply to it adequately. The relationship between the bank and the debtor is covered by the provision about the representation contract. The bank guarantee is a written declaration of the bank in the surety bond that the bank will satisfy the creditor up to the specific financial amount according to the security bond if a certain third person (debtor) does not fulfill his certain obligation or if other conditions according to the security bond are met. The bank gurantee can ensure:

- financial
- as well as not financial receivables, i.e. the financial claim, up to the amount set by the surety bond, of the creditor against the debtor in the case of the breach of the obligation covered by the bank guarantee.

The wording of the surety bond is absolutely decisive and the bank ensures the fulfillment of the obligation up to the amount and under conditions determined by the surety bond. This implies the following:

- the bank can assert toward the creditor only objections whose assertion is allowed by the surety bond, despite the fact that their assertion by the debtor toward the creditor would be otherwise possible;
- the previous call to the debtor asking him to fulfill his obligation is requested only if the surety bond provides so;
- if, according to the surety bond, the fulfillment of the bank based on the bank guarantee is conditioned by the presentation of certain documents, then these documents must be presented along with such a call or without any further delay after it;
- if, according to the surety bond, the validity time is limited, then the bank guarantee will expire if the creditor will not inform the bank in a written form about his claim from the bank guarantee during its validity time.

The bank will fulfill its obligation from the bank guarantee only if it is requested to do so by a written call from the creditor. After the bank has satisfied its duty according to the surety bond, the bank can ask the debtor to compensate it for what it has paid.

The acknowledgment of an obligation is an expression of the debtor´s will giving creedance to the existence of such an obligation in a certain extent. An obligation not statute-barred can be acknowledged in a written form as well as implicitly, i.e. by the payment of either interest or a part of the obligation. Contrariwise, the acknowledgment of an obligation which is already statute-barred requires a written form. A written acknowledgment of an obligation therefore:

- excludes the application of the objection of the statute-barred limitation, regardless whether the debtor knew about the statute-barred limitation at the moment of the acknowledgment of the obligation,
- starts a new statute-barred period in the length of four years from the day of the acknowledgment of the obligation;
- shifts the evidence burden in the case of the litigation from the creditor to the debtor.

The current regulation of the financial security in the Commercial Code is heavily influenced by the transposition of the European Law, especially the Directive of the European Parliament and Council 2000/12/EC from 20. March 2000 relating to the taking up and the pursuit of business of credit institutions (however, this Directive was rescinded with the effect on 20. July 2006). The concerned European regulation aims to create a regime for issuing order instruments and cash as securities in order to reinforce the integration, the stability of the financial market and the effectivness of the financial system of the E.U. The financial security under the Commercial Code includes the following:

- lien rights regarding financial collaterals agreed upon by the parties in order to ensure a financial receivable and

- transfer of a financial collateral for securing or other covering of a financial receivable.

The provider and accepter of the financial security can be, while observing conditions set by particular law acts, only:

- a bank;
- another Europan credit institution;
- insurance company, reinsurance company, businessman with order papers, investment company, investment fund or other financial institution subject matter to a supervison according to special law acts or to an international supervision;
- centra contra-party, settle accounter, clearing institution, or person performing a similar activity while doing business with derivates subject matter to a supervision according to special law acts or to an international supervision;
- savings or credit cooperative;
- person with a seat in a member state of the European Union or in another state from the European Economic Area allowed to issue electronic financial instruments and conducting business or doing activities in the territory of the Czech Republic based on a single licence in compliance with the European Law;
- the Czech Republic;
- autonomous regions, including similar foreign Public law persons;
- another country, including state institutions responsible for the management of public debt or conducting accounts of customers;
- the Czech National Bank;
- a foreign central bank;
- the European Central Bank;
- the International Monetary Fund;
- the European Investment Bank;
- the Bank for International Payments;
- the International Development Bank.

3.1.6 TERMINATION OF AN OBLIGATION

Typically, an obligation becomes extinct by its fulfillment. Nevertheless, the Commercial Code expressly regulates several specific situations when the termination occurs without the fulfillment of the obligation.

In the case of the termination of an obligation by the fulfillment, the termination occurs provided the creditor is satisfied duly and timely, i.e.:

- in a correct manner;
- in a correct extent
- in a correct place and
- in time or at least before the creditor withdraws from the contract.

If the obligation can be fulfilled in a number of different ways, the debtor has the right to determine the manner of the fulfillment, unless it implies from the contract that such a right belongs to the creditor. However, if the creditor does not determine this manner in a time set by the contract, otherwise until the time for the fulfillment, the debtor can determine the manner of the fulfillment.

If the fulfillment of the obligation is not tied to the personal characteristics of the debtor, the creditor must accept the fulfillment of the obligation offered by a third person, provided the debtor consents to it. The consent of the debtor is not required if the third person guarantees the obligation or otherwise assures that the debtor does not breach his obligation. Unless the relationship between the debtor and the third person implies otherwise, the third person enters by the fulfillment of the debtor's obligation into the creditor's rights and the creditor must give to such a third person all evidence generating instruments.

The creditor must accept even a partial fulfillment of the obligation provided such a partial fulfillment is not contradictory to the nature of the obligation or to the economic purpose followed by the creditor at the moment of the contract conclusion and such a purpose is expressed in the contract or was known to the debtor at the time of the conclusion. Similarly, when more obligations are fulfilled and the provided fulfillment does not satisfy all of them, the obligation designated by the debtor at the time of the fulfillment is considered to be fulfilled. If the debtor has more than one financial obligation toward the same creditor and the debtor does not designate which one is fulfilled, then the payment is deemed to go toward the non secured obligation or the obligation with the weakest securing, otherwise to the obligation first due and then first its accessories. The payment of a financial obligation goes first toward the interests and just then toward the principal, unless the debtor indicates otherwise.

To duly fulfill an obligation requires the fulfillment in a set place. According to a non-mandatory principle, only financial debts are portable. Therefore, in the case of the absence of the identificaiton of the place in the contract, and if it does not imply otherwise from the nature of the obligation, the debtor has to fulfill the obligation in the place where was his seat or his place of business or his domicile address, possibly his enterprise, at the time of the conclusion of the contract. A monetary obligation is fulfilled by a debtor on his risk and expenses in the seat, place of business or domicile address of the creditor, unless the contract or the Law states otherwise. A financial obligation can be fulfilled on the account of the creditor, conducted by a provider of financial services or through a post payment order, provided this does not contradict the financial terms agreed upon by the parties. The debtor must perform his obligation at the time set in the contract. If the time for the performance is not designated, then the creditor is allowed to request the performance of the obligation immediately after the conclusion of the contract and the debtor must perform the obligation without any unnecessary delay after he was asked for the performance by the creditor. Further, the mutuality of obligations is expected. Therefore, if it is not stated otherwise, in the case of reciprocal obligations one party can enforce the fulfillment of the obligation on the other party only if the enforcing party has already fulfilled its obligation or is ready to fulfill at the same time as the other party. If a debtor fulfills his financial obligation before the time set for the fulfillment, without a consent of the creditor, he is not allowed to subtract from the due amount the interest for a period of which the fulfillment occurred earlier.

When a debtor provides a defective performance and the creditor does not have the right to withdraw from the contract or the creditor does not use this right, the content of the obligation changes in the manner reflecting the claims of the creditor from the defective fulfillment and the obligation extincts with their satisfaction. A non perfect performance, i.e. a non duly and timely performed fulfillment, does not exclude the claim on compensation for damages and on contractual penalty.

Reciprocial and by the court enforceable receivables may extinct by a mutual crediting. A not yet due receivable cannot be credited toward a due receivable, unless it is a receivable against a debtor incapable to satisfy his monetary obligations. Monetary obligations in various currencies can be reciprocally credited only if the involved currencies are freely exchangeable. Parties have a large freedom to modify the above mentioned general regime of reciprocical crediting and can agree upon a reciprocical creditation of whatsoever receivables.

The termination of an obligation without a fulfillment occurs in the following cases:

- a withdrawal from the contract;
- a subsequent impossibility of performance;
- a payment of the agreed compensation for withdrawal from a contract and
- a frustration of the purpose of a contract.

A withdrawl from a contract is possible only if it is set by the contract or by the Commercial Code, which does so with respect to a due as well as future fulfillment. According to the Commercial Code, a withdrawal from a contract is possible even without an additional time period if the default of the debtor or creditor means a fundamental breach of a contractual duty and at the same time another party notifies about the withdrawal the party in default without any delay after such party has learnt about the default. A withdrawal in the case of a non fundamental breach needs to be preceeded by an expiration of an additional time period. In doubts, it is assumed that the breach is not fundamental. It is possible to withdraw from a contract involving a duty to be fulfilled in the future, if the behavior of the obligatorily party or other circumstances imply, even before the time set for the fulfillment of the contractual duty, that this duty will be breached in a significant manner and the obligatorily party does not extend, after a call from the beneficiary party, a sufficient security. The contract extincts through the withdrawal at the moment when the expression of the will of the beneficiary party is delivered to another party. Thereafter, the effects of the withdrawal cannot be revoked or modified without a consent of another party. The withdrawal from a contract extincts all contractual rights and duties. However, the withdrawal from a contract impacts neither the claim on a compensation for damages caused by the breach of contract nor the contractual clause regarding the selection of Law or of the regime of the Commercial Code (so called facultative or election businesses), regarding the dispute resolution or other provision which, due to the expressed will of partes or due to their nature, should last even after the termination of the contract.

Another reason for the termination of an obligation without its fulfillment, aside from the withdrawal, is the fact that the obligation becomes objectively not performable, i.e. the obligation can be fulfilled neither by the debtor nor by someone else. The theory did not consider the consequent illegality of the fulfillment for a consequent impossibility, the Commercial Code does so. Therefore, the Commercial Code includes factual subsequent impossibilities as well as legal subsequent impossibilities. The impossibility of the fulfillment needs to be proven by the debtor. The debtor whose duty has extincted due to the impossibility of fulfillment, has to compensate the creditor for the caused damage unless the impossibility of the fulfillment has been caused by circumstances excluding the responsibility.

The compensation for withdrawal from a contract is a contractual arrangement according to which one contractual party or all contractual parties are allowed to cancel the contract through the payment of an amount called a compensation for withdrawal from a contract. The concerned contract extincts *ex tunc* (retroactively back from its conclusion) with the delivery of the notification about the application of the withdrawal clause and the payment of the compensation. The involved contract is cancelled *ex tunc* with the delivery of the notification and the payment of the compensation for withdrawal, i.e. the contract disappears as if it has never existed. Therefore, claims on compensation for damage or on payment of a contractual penalty for the breach of contractual duties are excluded. Therefore, the compensation for the withdrawal from a contract constitutes a contractual instrument creating the possibility to terminate an obligation without engaging a liability and protecting, resp. securing, interests of both parties. During their negotiation about the compensation for withdrawal from a contract and its enforcement, the contractual parties are limited only by the general duty to maintain the principle of honest business conduct and the specific duty not to execute the fulfillment under the contract, i.e. the party which has accepted the contractual fulfillment (or it´s part) or which has provided another party with the fulfillment (or it´s part) can not cancel the contract through the payment of the agreed compensation for withdrawal from the contract. The frustration of the purpose of a contract is close to the impossibility of the fulfillment and underlies to a similar regime. The defeat of the basic and expressly mentioned purpose due to a fundamental change of circumstances after the conclusion of the contract allows the concerned party to withdraw from a contract. The most frequent case is a legal event which does not need to have for a consequence the impossibility of the performance but which means an impossibility to reach the contractual purpose. In order to stabilize the relationships and to reduce the speculative abuses of withdrawal, the change in the economic situation of one party or the change of an economic or market situation is not considered to be a fundamental change.

3.1.7 BREACH OF CONTRACTUAL DUTIES

The breach of contractual duites can be caused by the debtor as well as by the creditor. In both cases, it can create a claim on compensation for the damage caused to another party. The breaching party or the party which, while considering all the circumstances should know that it will breach the contract, has to inform the other party about it. Simultaneously, the party informed about the breach or the party threatened by a damage has to arrange for all measures to avoid or at least to reduce the damage. The breach per se makes the shift of the risk of damage on the concerned item (for it´s loss, it´s destruction or it´s value deterioration). However, the very obligation to duly and timely fulfill does not extinct and the withdrawal is possible only if it is agreed on or provided for by the law.

The breach of contractual duties occurs when the debtor does not fulfill its obligation duly and timely, with the exception of the case of the impossibility of performance of the obligation due to the creditor. If the debtor is in default with the satisfaction with a monetary obligation or it´s part and the default interest is not agreed upon, then the debtor has to be paid from the due amount the interests determined by the Civil law, i.e. annual default interests in the amount of the repo rate determined by the Czech National Bank increased by 7% points. If the due date or the payment term is not set by the contract, the claim on the default interest arises without the need of a reminder:

- the expiration of 30 days from the day when the debtor received the invoice or a similar request for payment,
- if the day of the receipt of the invoice or of the similar request for payment cannot be determined, then after the expiration of 30 days after the receipt of goods or services,
- if the debtor receives the invoice or a similar request for payment before the delivery of goods or services, then after the expiration of 30 days after the receipt of such goods or services, or
- if the Law or the contract orders the acceptance or the confirmation of the comformity of goods or services with the contract and if the debtor receives the invoice or a similar request for payment before or at the moment of the acceptance or at the moment of the confirmation of the the comformity, then after the expiration of 30 days after such a later date.

The creditor has a claim on a compensation for damages caused by the default with the fulfillment of a monetary obligation only if such a damage is not covered by the default interests.

The creditor is in default when, contrary to his duties under his contractual duties, he fails to accept a duly offered fulfillment or does not extend the collaboration necessary for the debtor to fulfill his obligation. The withdrawal from a contract is possible only in cases set by the Law or by the contract. If neither the Law nor the contract provides otherwise, then the debtor may demand from the creditor in default the fulfillment of his duty along with the compensation for the damage.

Therefore, regardless if it is caused by a debtor or by a creditor, the compensation for the caused damage is provided for except in cases when it is proven that it was caused by circumstances excluding the responsibility. The following obstacles are considered as such circumstances:

- it was unforeseeable at the time of the creation of the obligation,
- it has arisen independently from the will of the obligatory party,
- in the period of default,
- it hinders the party in the fulfillment of his obligation,
- it´s avertment by the obligatory party cannot be reasonably expected,
- and it does depend upon the economic situation.

In principle, the real damage and the lost profit, i.e. the profit usually reached in the honest business conduct under conditions similar to those of the breached contract in the given business area. The damage exceeding the damage which the obligatory party at the time of the creation of the obligation could expect or which may be expected while considering the facts known or should be known with a standard care. The compensation of the damage in money is preferred. Only if the beneficiary party requests and it is possible, then the damage is compensated by the return into the previous status. It is impossible to resign on the claim on the damage compensaton before the breach of the duty from which the damage arises. The damage compensation cannot be moderated by the court.

If more persons are bound to the compensation of the damage, then these people are bound jointly and severally, and they will settle with each other according to the extent of their responsibility.

3.1.8 Statute of limitations

The Czech Public as well as Private Law includes the statute of limitations and therefore it applies across to the Czech legal regime that the rights can be barred by the expiration of a period by the statute of limitations. All rights from commercial obligations are a subject matter to the statute of limitation except of the right on termination notice regarding a contract for an undetermined period. The change in the person of the debtor or of the creditor does not have any influence on the run of the statute of limitation period. After the expiration of the statute of limitation period the rights do not extinct, but the obligatory party can raise an objection regarding the statute of limitations and so avoid the recognition of the rights by the court. However, if the obligatory party performs its obligation after the expiration of the statute limitation period, then such a party cannot consequently request the return of the fulfillment.

In principle, the statute of limitations period starts with the due date, i.e. for rights enforceable with courts from the date when the claim could be filed with the court. For rights to perform a legal act, the statute of limitations period starts on the day when the legal act could have been performed. For rights on partial fulfillment, the statute of limitation period runs for each partial fulfillment separately. For rights for the defects of goods, the statute of limitation period starts on the day of their transmission to the beneficiary or other determined person from the day when the duty to transmit has been breached. For claims from the guarantee for the quality, the statute of limitation period runs from the day of the timely default notification during the guarantee period and for claims from the legal defects from their enforcement by a third person.

The length of the general statute of limitations period under the Commercial Code is one year longer than the length of the general statute of limitation period under the Civil Code. Therefore, claims from commercial obligations are statute barred after four years, unless provided otherwise. For the right on a compensation for damage, the statute of limitation period starts on the day when the damaged person did learn or should have learned about the damage and about the person responsible to provide the compensation. However, this period cannot pass beyond ten years from the day when the breach of duty occurred.

The statute of limitation period ceased to run when the creditor starts a court proceedings or arbitration proceedings to claim his rights or during such proceedings use his rights as contra-claim. In any case, the statute of limitation period ends, at the latest, after ten years from the day when it started to run.

The party against whom the right is subject to the statute of limitation can, by a written declaration toward the other party, extend the statute of limitation period, even repeatedly. Nevertheless, the total statute of limitation period cannot exceed ten years from the day when it started to run for the first time. Such a declaration can be made even before the start of the statute of limitation period. At the written acknowledgment of an obligation by the debtor, it triggers a new statute of limitation period in the extent of four years. The payment, even partial, of a debt or of it´s interest, is deemed to be an acknowledgment of obligation as well.

3.2 SPECIAL REGULATION OF SELECTED COMMERCIAL OBLIGATIONS

3.2.1 SALES CONTRACT

The Commercial Code regulates the sales contract regarding the sale of movable things and items. Therefore, the sale of immovables (real estates) belongs to the exclusive regime of the Civil Code (with the exception of the sale of an enterprise).

The sales contract according to the Commercial Code establishes:

- an obligation of the seller to deliver an existing or a future movable thing specified individually or at least in kind and quantity along with necessary or by contract requested documents and transfer on him the ownership right;

- an obligation of the buyer to pay the agreed sales price or a price which can be determined according to the agreed mechanism (e.g., the price clause) and take over the delivered things according to the contract.

A contract under which a dominant part of the obligation of the seller consists either of conducting activites or assembling (see Chapter 3.2.6 Contract for Work), then such a contract is not deemed to be a sales contract. If the negotiation about the conclusion of a contract implies a will to conclude a sales contract without any determination of the sales price, then the sales contract is valid and the buyer has to pay the sales price for what similar merchandise has been sold under similar contractual terms at the time of the contract conclusion.

Generally, the fulfillment from the sales contract is provided by the seller. Unless the parties agree otherwise, then the handing over of the merchandise is realized when the merchandise is given to the 1st transportor transporting it to the buyers or by allowing the buyer to dispose with the merchandise at the place of the buyer or at the place where the merchandise is to be found.

The seller has a duty to hand over the merchandise in the terms set by the contract. If the seller hands over the merchandise earlier, the buyer has a right to either take over it or refuse it. If the term of the handing over of the merchandise is not set by the contract, then the seller has to hand over the merchandise to the buyer without any notice and in a reasonable time considering the nature of the merchandise and the place of the delivery. Unless business customs or previous established practices between parties implies otherwise, the below contractual terms are understood for the purposes of the determination of the time of the fulfillment as follows:

- "beginning of the period" means the first 10 days of the period,
- "in the middle of the month" means between the 10th and 20th day of the month,
- "in the middle of the trimester" means the 2nd month of the trimester,

- "the end of the period" means the last 10 days of the period,
- "immediately" means for the food-stuffs and raw stuffs within two days, for machineries 10 days, and for the remaining merchandise 5 days.

The period of the fulfillment can be followed by a probation period based on the clause, about the sale upon approval, agreed by parties. The buyer has a three months period or other agreed period for the approval of the merchandise. If the buyer did not take over the merchandise, it is a condition precedent. This condition is considered defeated when the buyer does not inform the seller during the probation time about his approval of the merchandise. Contrariwise, the taking over of the merchandise transforms this condition into a condition of cancellation and it is assumed that the buyer approved the merchanidise if he does not refuse it in writing and during the probation period. In both cases, the buyer does not have the right to refuse the merchandise if he cannot return it in the same shape as he got it.

The seller has to deliver the merchandise:

- without any legal defects (no claims of a third person unless the seller has agreed to such a restriction),
- in the quality, in the quantity and in the design as determined by the contract, and
- he must package or prepare it for the transfer as defined by the contract.

When the nature of the merchandise implies that the quantity designated by the contract is just approximate, the difference between the quantity of the merchandise designated in the contract and the quantity of the merchandise really delivered can be at the upper most 5% of the quantity designated in the contract, unless the contract, the established practice between parties or from the previous practice between parties or business customs do not imply otherwise. In the lack of the contractual regulation, the seller has to package the merchandise and deliver it in the manner, in the quality and in the design, which are usual and matches the purpose set by the contract.

When the seller breaks his above duty to deliver the merchandise, the merchandise has defects. The delivery of some other merchandise than was indicated by the contract, and/or mistakes in the documents necessary for using the merchandise, means the problems are considered the defects of the merchandise. The seller is not responsible for defects of the merchandise which were known to the buyer at the time of the conclusion of the contract or which the buyer must know considering the circumstances around the conclusion of the contract, unless these defects concern a quality of the merchandise stipulated by the contract. The seller is responsible for defects which the merchandise has at the time of the transfer of risk on the merchandise from the seller on to the buyer, even if the defect becomes obvious later on. The seller's duties from the quality warranty are not impacted by this.

The buyer has to inspect the merchandise as soon as possible after the transfer of risk on the merchandise, while considering the nature of the merchandise.

If the contract provides for the shipment of the merchandise to the buyer, the inspection can be postponed until the time when the merchandise is delivered to the designated place. If the buyer neither inspects nor arranges for inspection of the merchandise at the time of the transfer of risk, he can claim defects which could have been discovered during the inspection only if he proves that the merchandise had them at the time of the transfer of risk. The claim of the buyer cannot be recognized in a court proceeding if the buyer does not provide a notice to the seller about the defects in the merchandise without any unnecessary delay after:

- the buyer discovered the defect,
- the buyer could have discovered the defects during the inspection while extending professional care,
- the defects could have been discovered later while extending professional care, at the latest within two years from the delivery of the merchandise, or from the arrival of the merchandise at the place designated by the contract,
- for defects covered by the warranty, the warranty period is used instead.

The quality warranty is a written obligation of the seller that the delivered merchandise will be, for a certain period, apt to be used to the purpose stated in the contract, otherwise to a usual purpose, or that it will maintain the qualities stated by the contract, otherwise usual qualities. The quality warranty can be implied from the contract, from the warranty deed or from the indication of warranty period or lifespan period or usueable period of the merchandise on it´s package.

Claims from defects of the merchandise depends upon the degrese of the breach of the contract. If the delivery of the merchandise with defects breaches the contract in a fundamental manner, the buyer can request:

- a defects clearance through the delivery of substituted merchandise instead of the defective merchandise, missing merchandise and removing legal defects,
- a defects clearance through the merchandise reparation, provided the defects are reparable,
- an appropriate sales price reduction;
- a withdrawal from the contract.

The choice between these claims belongs to the buyer only if he informs the seller about it in a timely sent notice or without any unnecessary delay after the notice. The applied claim cannot be changed by the buyer without the seller´s consent. Naturally, aside from this claim or these claims, the buyer has a claim on the compensation for damages and a contractual penalty, provided it was agreed upon.

If the delivery of the merchandise with defects breaches the contract in a non fundamental manner, the buyer can request:

- a delivery of the missing merchandise,
- a clearance of other defects,
- an appropriate sales price reduction.

If the buyer requests the defects clearance, he cannot, before the expiration of an additional appropriate term, which the buyer needs to provide him with for such a purpose, set up other claims from the defects of the merchandise, except from the claim on a compensation of damages and a contractual penalty, unless the seller informs the buyer that he will not satisfy his duty in the term. If the seller does not clear the defects of the merchandise in the term, the buyer can claim the sales price reduction or withdraw from the contract, provided he informs the buyer about his intention to withdraw from the contract while setting the period or in an appropriate time before the contract withdrawal. The selected claim cannot be changed by the buyer without the consent of the seller.

Claims from the defects of the merchandise are exclusive, i.e. they are not to be substituted with claims on compensation for damage or with claims on contractual penalty. They do not have any impact on the compensation for damage or on the contractual penalty. Further, the buyer having a claim on the sales price reduction is not entitled to request a compensation for the lost profit as a consequence of the defect of the merchandise covered by such a sales price reduction.

If the parties do not agree otherwise, the buyer acquires the ownership right to the merchandise with the handing over of the delivered merchandise or when he is allowed to dispose with the delivery. The buyer acquires the ownership right even in the case when the seller is not the owner of the sold merchandise, unless at the time of the expected acquisition of the ownership the buyer knew or should have known that the seller is not the owner and is not entitled to dispose with the merchandise for the purpose of its sale.

Unless the stipulation of the ownership reserve implies otherwise, it is assumed that the buyer should acquire the ownership right only after the full payment of the sales price. Simultaneously, the buyer does not need to pay the sales price before he is allowed to inspect the merchandise unless the agreed manner of the delivery of the merchandise or of the payment of the sales price would be in contradiction with it. The risk of damage of the merchandise passes on to the buyer when he takes over the merchandise from the seller or, if he does not do so in a timely manner, when the seller allows him to dispose with the merchandise and the buyer breaches the contract by the failure to take over the merchandise.

3.2.2 RENT AND SALE CONTRACT REGARDING AN ENTERPRISE

Since the Commercial Code sets a special regime for contracts having for their subject matter an enterprise, the determination of the enterprise is important. In general, the enterprise means a collection of:

- tangible parts for entrepreunership (e.g., pieces of land, buildings, equipment, machineries);
- intangibles parts for entrepreunership (e.g., intellectual property) and
- personal parts for entrepreneurship (e.g., the structure, the composition and the level of employees and cooperating people).
- The enterprise is a bulk item and includes items, rights and other ownership values which belong to the entrepreneur and serve for the operation of an enterprise or which, due to their nature, should serve to such a purpose.

By the rent contract regarding an enterprise

- the landlord commits to leave his enterprise to a tenant in order that the tenant could independently operate and manage on his own expenses and risk and could collect the profit out of it, and
- the tenant commits to pay rent to the landlord.

The rent contract regarding an enterprise must be concluded in a written form, be published through its filing in the collections of deeds of the commercial register and include either the amount of rent or the manner of its determination. The enterprise cannot be sub-leased. The tenant can be only the entrepreneur registered in the commercial register which has an appropriate business license, otherwise the rent contract is invalid. The tenant must operate the enterprise with professional care, and without the consent of the landlord, is not allowed to change the subject of the business operated in the rent enterprise. The rights and duties belonging to the rent enterprise pass to the tenant at the moment of the effectivity of the rent contract. This applies as well to rights and duties from the labor relations. The tenant guarantees for obligations belonging to the enterprise and which have arisen before the effectivity of the rent contract. The tenant operates the rent enterprise under its firm denomination. If the rent contract regarding an enterprise has been concluded for an undetermined time, a party can withdraw from it at latest six months before the expiration of the accounting period to the last day of the accounting period, unless the rent contract provides for another withdrawal notice period. For the time of the rent, a non competition clause can restrict the activitiy of the landlord and after the termination of the rent, a competiton clause can restrict the activity of the tenant.

By the sales contract regarding an enterprise

- the seller commits to hand over to the buyer the enterprise and transfer to him the ownership right to the enterprise and
- the buyer commits to take over the obligations related to the enterprise from the seller and pay the sales price.

Similarly to the rent contract regarding an enterprise, the sales contract regarding an enterprise must be concluded in a written form. In addition, if the parts of the enterprise are real estates, which is highly likely in the praxis, then they need to be exactly specified for the purpose of the real estates cadastre and further the expression of parties′ will needs to be at the same page, i.e. the parties must put their signatures on the same page. If the enterprise is sold by a person registered in the commercial register, he will request the registration of the sales of the enterprise or its part into the commercial register. The buyer acquires all rights and duties, including those from labor relations of employees of the enterprise. The transfer of obligations does not require any consent of creditors and the seller guarantees to the buyer that they will be satisfied. The buyer has to notify creditors about the transmission of all obligations without any unnecessary delay and the seller has to notify all debtors about the transmission of all receivables to the buyer. The non competition clause may restrict the activity of the seller. The sales price is determined based on data about the sum of items, rights and duties kept in the accounting records related to the sold enterprise on the day of the conclusion of the sales contract and based on other values mentioned by the sales contract which are not included in the accounting records. If the sales contract should become effective on a later day, the sales price changes in consideration of the increase or of the decrease of the assets which has occurred in the meantime. The buyer has a right on an appropriate sales price reduction regarding obligations which have passed on him and were not included in the accounting records at the time of the effectivness of the sales contract, unless the buyer knew about them at the time of the conclusion of the sales contract. On the day of the effectiveness of the sales contract, the seller has to hand over and the buyer has to take items included in the sales. The transmission is a subject matter of a protocol signed by both parties. With the transmission of items passes the risk of damage from the seller to the buyer. The ownership right to the items which are included in the sale passes to the buyer with the effectiveness of the contract. The ownership right to real estates passes with the registration in the real estate cadastre. The buyer is allowed to withdraw from the sales contract if the enterprise is not fit to the operation designated in the contract and defects timely notified are not reparable or the seller does not clear them in an appropriate additional time given to him for it by the seller. It does not concern a general unfitness to the operation but only to the unfitness to the operation under the sales contract. Further, the buyer can withdraw if the ownership right to a real estate, which is a part of an enterprise, does not pass to him and the seller does not clear this defect in an appropriate additional time.

3.2.3 SALES CONTRACT FOR A LEASED GOOD

The sales contract for a leased good is similar, but not identical, to the leasing. The difference consists of the fact that the leasing is not one contract but always a combination of several mutually depending contracts involving three parties. The leasing is close to the loan or credit and generally is understood as a "technique for financing with a real security." In the Czech Republic, the operations of leasing not oriented toward the acquisition of the ownership and the financial leasing oriented toward the acquisition of the ownership belong to the the basic leasing types.

Through the sales contract for a leased good, the contractual parties agree in the rent contract, or after its conclusion, that upon a written notification the tenant is allowed to buy the leased good or the leased collection of goods during the validity of the rent contract or after its termination. Similar to the rent and sales contract regarding an enterprise, the sales contract for a leased good requires a written form.

Upon the delivery of the written notification about the purchase of the leased movable item, the risk of loss and the ownership pass to the buyer. The ownership right to real estates passes upon the registration with the real estate cadastre.

If neither the sales price decisive for the application of the right to buy the leased good nor the manner of its determination is designated in the agreement, the buyer has to pay a sales price for which typically is sold such a merchandise or a comparable merchandise at the time of the conclusion of the contract. The alteration or deterioration of the good, for which is responsible the tenant, does not have any influence on the sales price determination. The buyer must pay the sales price without any unnecessary delay after the creation of the sales contract. If the parties agree that, during a certain period of the validity of the rent contract, the tenant is allowed to acquire the ownership right to the leased good for free, then the determination of the sales price and its payment fall off.

For consideration of defects of the good are decisive qualities which should have had the leased good. The period to notify the defects of the bought and previously leased good are calculated from the day when the tenant took over the leased good.

3.2.4 CREDIT CONTRACT

By the credit contract, the creditor commits to provide to a debtor, upon his request, with a financial amount and the debtor commits to return the provided financial amount and to pay the interest. Unless the parties agree otherwise, the debtor has to return the financial amount in the currency in which he received it and to pay in the same currency the interests. If the credit contract does not stipulate another withdrawal period, the debtor can withdraw from the credit contract with an immediate effect and the creditor by the end of the next calendar month following the month of the delivery of the notice to the debtor.

It is possible to agree upon a price for the agreement on the obligation of the creditor to provide upon request a financial amount, if providing credits is a subject of the business activities of the creditor. The creditor has to provide the agreed upon financial amount when the debtor requests him for it according to the credit contract and this in the time indicated by the request, otherwise without any unnecessary delay. The debtor has to return the provided amount in the agreed period, otherwise in one month from the day when he was asked for the return by the creditor.

The debtor has to pay the agreed upon interests on the amount from the time it was provided. If the interests are not agreed upon, the debtor has to pay interests usual for credits which are extended by banks in the place of the seat of the debtor in the time of the conclusion of the credit contract. If the parties agree upon the interest exceeding the highest allowable amount of interests provided by the law or based on the law, then the debtor has to pay the interests in the highest allowable amount.

The interests are due along with the obligation to return the provided financial amount. If the period to return the provided financial amount is longer than one year, the interests are due at the end of each calendar year. The debtor is allowed to return the provided financial amount before the time set by the credit contract. He has to pay interests only for the time from the providing to the return of the financial amount.

If the security of the obligation to return the financial amount extincts or deteriorates during the validity of the credit contract, the debtor has to complete the security unto the original extent. If the debtor does not do so in an appropriate time, the creditor can withdraw from the contract and request the debtor to return the owing amount along with interest. In addition, the creditor can withdraw from the credit contract and request the return of the owing amount with interests if the debtor is behind with the return of more then two installment payments or one installment payment for more than three months and if the debtor uses the financial amount for some other purpose than was agreed upon. The withdrawal of the creditor from the credit contract does not have any impact on the security of the obligation from the credit contract.

3.2.5 Licence Agreement Regarding Industrial Property

By the licence agreement regarding industrial property the licensor allows the licensee to the exercise of industrial property rights within the agreed territory and the licensee commits to pay a certain fee or other asset value. Similar to the rent and sales contract regarding an enterprise, the sales contract for a leased good, the licence agreement regarding industrial property requires a written form.

This contract is used for patents on inventions, for utility models, for industrial designs, for trademarks, for topographic on semi-conduct products, for new plant species and animal breeds. The exercise of rights provided based on such a licence agreement requires a registration in the register kept regarding the given subject of the industrial property (notably the register kept by the Office of industrial property in Prague).

The licensor has to provide the licensee with all documentation and information needed for the exercise of the rights under the agreement without any unnecessary delay after the conclusion of the agreement.

The licensor may continue to exercise the rights which are the object of the licence agreement and may also grant it to other persons. Contrariwise, the sub-licensing is prohibited, i.e. the licensee is not allowed to grant the rights to other persons.

The licensee must keep confidential the provided documentation and information with respect to third persons, unless the license agreement or the nature of the provided documentation and information imply that the licensor is not interested in keeping them confidential. A person participating in the business activity of the entrepreneur and bound by the entrepreneur to maintain confidentiality is not considered to be a third person. The licensee has to return the provided documentation after the termination of the licence agreement and continue to keep confidential the information until they will become generally known.

If the license agreement has not been concluded for a determined period, it may be terminated by a notice. If the license agreement does not stipulate another notice period, the notice becomes effective after the expiration of one year from the end of the calendar month when the notice was delivered to another party.

3.2.6 CONTRACT FOR WORK

By the contract for work, the contractor commits himself to execute a certain work, i.e. to its termination and delivery, and the client commits himself to pay a price for it. The work means:

- the creation of a certain good unless it falls within the scope of a sales contract,
- the assembly of a certain good,
- the maintenance of a certain good,
- the performance of a repair or modification of a certain good,
- the material expression of a result of another activity.

An assembly, maintaince, repair or modification of a building or its part is always a work.

The price must be always agreed upon in the contract or the manner of its determination must be indicated in the contract, unless the negotiation about the conclusion of the contract implies the will of parties to conclude the contract without this indication. The price can be determined according to a budget. The client has to pay the price in the time agreed in the contract, otherwise when the work is executed.

The contractor must execute the work:

- independently, unless he committed himself expressly to follow the client's instructions,
- at his own costs,
- at his risk,
- in the agreed time, otherwise in an appropriate time considering the nature of the work.

The contractor can delegate the execution of the work to another person, unless the contract or the nature of the work contradicts it. When the work is executed by a delegated person, the contractor remains responsible for it as if the work were executed by him.

Regarding the items purchased by the contractor for the execution of the work, the contractor is considered to be in a position similar to the seller, unless the provisions about the contractor for work does not state otherwise. He carries the risk of damage on them and remains their owner until they are incorporated into the work. In doubts, it is assumed that the purchased price of these items is included in the price for work. Regarding the entrusted items, the contractor is considered to be in a position similar to the position of the warehouse-keeper.

If the contractor executes a work by the client, on his piece of land or a piece of land which the client supplied, the client carries the risk of damage on the executed work and is its owner unless the contract for work states otherwise. In other cases, except for the maintenance, repair, and modification of an item, the contractor carries the risk of damage on the created work and is its owner. The provisions about passing the risk of danger from the seller to the buyer are applied by the transition of the risk of danger on the work from the contractor on to the client.

The client is allowed to control the execution of the work. The contractor has to notify the client without any unnecessary delay about an unfit nature of items handed over by the client or client's instructions for the contractor without any unnecessary delay, unless the contractor could have discovered such an unfit nature while exercising professional care. If the contract stipulates that the client is allowed to control the work on a certain degree of execution, the contractor has to invite the client in a timely manner to control it.

With the handing over of the work starts the warranty period and the client acquires to the executed work the ownership right, if until then it has been held by the contractor, and the risk of damage on the work passes to the client, if until then it has been carried by the contractor. If any of the parties requires it, a protocol about the transmission of the work is drafted and signed by both parties.

The client has to inspect the work or arrange for the inspection of the work as soon as possible after the transmission of the work. The court does not acknowledge to the client rights from defects on the work if the client has not given notice about these defects of the work without any unnecessary delay.

The work has defects if its execution does not correspond with the result designated in the contract. The contractor is responsible for defects which the work has at the time of the transmission. However, if the risk of damage on the created work passes on to the client later, the time of such transmission is decisive. Regarding the defects covered by the quality warranty, the contractor is responsible in the extent of such a quality warranty.

3.2.7 REPRESENTATION CONTRACT

By the representation contract, the respresentative commits himself so that, for a remuneration, he will arrange at the client's expense a certain business matter by performing legal acts in the name of the client or by performing some other activity and the client commits himself to pay the representative a remuneration for it. The respresentative is not responsible for the breach of the obligation by the person with whom he concluded a contract during the arranging of the business matter, unless the representation contract states that he is liable for the fulfillment of obligations taken over by other persons relating to the arrangement for the matter. The client can at any time give a notice regarding the entire representation contract or its part. The representative can give a notice with the effectiveness to the end of the calendar month following the month when the notice was delivered to the client, unless the notice implies a longer notice period. The obligation of the representative expires with his death in the case of physical persons or with the termination in the case of legal persons.

The representative must:

- perform while extending the professional care;
- follow the clients' instructions;
- follow the clients' interests,
- notify the client about all circumstances which he discovered while performing within the matter and which might have influence on the modification of the client's instructions;
- arrange the matter personally only if the representation contract states so, and
- transmit to the client items which he took over while arranging for the matter without any unnecessary delay.

The client must:

- transmit in a timely manner to the representative all needed items and information;
- issue in a timely manner a power of attorney in a written form for the representative if he arranges matters by performing legal acts in the name of the client.

The representantive is liable for damages on items handed over from the client for the arrangement of the business matter or on items handed over to him by third persons during the arrangement of the business, unless he could not have avoided the damage despite extending the professional care.

If the amount of the remuneration is not mentioned in the representation contract, the client has to pay to the representative a remuneration which is usual at the time of the conclusion of the representation contract for an activity similar to the activity performed by the representative while arranging for the business matter.

If the representation contract does not state otherwise, the claim of the representative on the remuneration arises when the due activity has been duly performed, regardless whether it brought the expected result or not. The client has to reimburse the necessary and useful expenses of the represantative unless their nature implies that they are already included in ther remuneration.

3.2.8 COMMISSION AGENT'S CONTRACT

By the commission agent's contract, the agent commits himself to arrange in his own name but at the principal's account a certain business matter for the principal and the principal commits himself to pay him a commission.

The agent has to:

- act with due professional care;
- follow the principal's instructions (he can diverge from them only if it is in the principal's interest and he can obtain a timely consent);
- protect all to him known client's interests related to the arrangement of the business matter;
- inform the principal about all circumstances which could have an influence regarding the change of the principal instructions;
- provide the principal with reports about the arrangement of the business matter in the manner set by the commission agent's contract, otherwise upon a principal's request;
- provide the principal with a report about the result after having arranged for the business matter;

- to render unto him the accounts, and
- to transfer on the principal all rights acquired during the arrangement of the business matter without any unnecessary delay and give him all what the agent has obtained during his activity and the client has a duty to take it over.

Agent´s acts do not create any relationships between the principal and third persons or any rights or duties of the principal. However, the principal can request from a third person a handing over of an item or a fulfillment of an obligation, which was arranged for him by the agent, if the agent cannot do so due to circumstances concerning the agent. The principal remains the owner of movable items conveyed to the agent until their acquisition by a third person. The agent is liable for damage on such items as a warehouse-keeper. The principal acquires the ownership to movable items acquired for him by the agent at the moment of their transmission to the agent.

If the person, with whom the agent concluded a contract while arranging for the business matter, breaches his obligations, the agent has to enforce the fulfillment of these obligations on the account of the principal or, if the principal agrees to it, assign to him a receivable corresponding to these obligations.

In contrast to the representation contract, for which the spent effort is decisive, the commission agent´s contract stresses the result, i.e. the obligation of the agent to achieve a certain result (similar to the contract for work). Therefore, the claim on the remuneration arises only after the fulfillment of the obligation and if the amount has not been agreed upon, then the remuneration appropriate to the performed activity and the reached result. The contractual parties can modify this regulation of the Commercial Code and agree e.g. upon a payment of an advance payment or consecutive partial payments. The client has to pay along with the remuneration the expenses of the agent which were spent necessarily and usefully while the agent was sastisfying his obligation. In doubts, it is assumed that the remuneration includes the compensation of these expenses.

3.2.9 INTERMEDIATION CONTRACT

By the intermediation contract, the intermediary commits himself to develop an activity leading to generating an opportunity for the client to conclude a certain contract with a third person and the client commits himself to pay a fee for it to the intermediary.

The intermediary has to inform the client without any unnecessary delay about all circumstances important for the client´s decision making regarding the conclusion of the intermediated contract and has to keep a documentation, which he has acquired during his intermediation activity, for the client´s needs. This documentation keeping duty lasts as long as the documentation may be important for the protection of the client´s interests. The client has to inform the intermediary about all information which can be decisive for the conclusion of the contract.

The intermediary does not guarantee the fulfillment of obligations of third persons with whom the contract was concluded. However, the intermediary must not suggest to the client a conclusion of an intermediated contract with a person about whom the intermediary knows or should have known that there is a justified doubt about a due and timely fulfillment of the obligation from the intermediated contract.

The intermediary has a claim on an agreed fee, otherwise a claim on a fee usual for the intermediation of   similar intermediated contracts at the time of the conclusion of the intermediation contract.

If the basis for the determination of the fee is the extent of the fulfillment of the obligation of a third person, the fulfillment not provided due to reasons on the side of the client is included in such a basis.

The intermediary has a claim upon the reimbursement of expenses related to the intermediation only if such a reimubrsement is expressly agreed upon and, in doubts, only if the intermediary has a claim as well on the fee.

The claim of the intermediary on the fee arises:

- by the conclusion of the intermediated contract;
- already by the arrangement of the opportunity for the client to conclude the intermediated contract with a third person, provided the intermediaton contract stipulates so;
- only after the fulfillment of the obligation of the third person, provided the intermediation contract stipulates so.

The claim of the intermediary on the fee is not hindered by the fact that the intermediated contract is concluded, or possibly fulfilled, only after the expiration of the intermediation contract. On the contrary, the claim of the intermediary does not arise if the intermediated contract with a third person has been concluded without any intermediary ´s contribution or if in the breach of the intermediation contract the intermediary has been active as well for the third person concluding the intermediated contract.

The intermediation contract expires if the intermediated contract is not concluded in the period designated by the intermediation contract. If such a period is not designated by the intermediation contract, each party can terminate the intermediation contract by notifying the other party.

3.2.10 COMMERCIAL REPRESENTANTION CONTRACT

By the commercial representation contract, the commercial representative as an independent entrepreneur commits himself for a commission to engage in a long-term activity on behalf of the principal aimed at the conclusion of specified contracts or to negotiate and conclude a transaction in the name of the principal and on his account. Similar to the rent and sales contract regarding an enterprise, the sales contract for a leased good or license agreement, the commercial representation contract must be concluded in a written form. The exclusivity is not assumed and therefore it must be expressly agreed upon. Otherwise the principal can delegate his commercial representation to some other persons and the commercial representative can conduct activities that are the subject matter of the agreed commercial representation as well for other persons or conclude business transactions which are the subject matter of the agreed upon commercial representation on his account or an other person's account.

The commercial representative cannot be:

- a person able as a corporate body to bind a legal person,
- an associate or a member empowered by the law to bind other associates or members,
- a liquidator,
- a bankruptcy manager, or
- persons acting on the Czech or foreign regulated market or in a Czech or foreign multi-party commercial system or commodity stock-exchange.

The commercial representative must:

- act in a long term and within the agreed upon territory (if such a territory is not designated, then within the territory of the Czech Republic),
- act honestly, with due care and in good faith,
- follow the principal's interests and observe the limits of the delegation and reasonable instructions of the principal,
- search for intereseted persons to conclude certain business transactions,
- provide the principal with necessary information which he has,
- inform the principal about the market evolution and all circumstances necessary for the principal's interest, especially for his decision making regarding the business transactions to be concluded,
- conduct other activities leading to business transactions in the name of the principal and on his account,

- co-operate with the solution of discrepancies arising from the concluded business transactions,
- without any unnecessary delay inform the principal about his incapacity to conduct the agreed activity, and
- return all documentation, instruments and documents to the principal after the expiration of the commercial representation contract.

Without a conferred power of attorney, the commercial representative is not allowed to conclude business transactions in the name of the principal or to accept whatsoever for him or to do other legal acts. Further, the commercial representative must not communicate any information acquired from the principal for his activity without the consent of the principal to third persons or to use them for himself or for other persons, if this would be in breach of the interests of the principal. This duty lasts after the expiration of the commercial representation contract.

The principal must:

- act honestly and in good faith,
- hand over all documentation, instruments and necessary documents for the fulfillment of the commercial representative obligations,
- provide the commercial representative with information necessary for the fulfillment of the commercial representative obligations,
- inform the commercial representative in a timely manner about his acceptance or declination or non-satisfaction of an act arranged for by the commercial representative,
- pay the agreed upon commission, and, if the amount has not been designated, then a commission corresponding to the customs of the place of the activity and while taking into account the nature of the merchandise (in the case of the lack of customs, a commission in a reasonable amount is to be paid),
- if agreed upon, reimburse, along with the commission, as well the expenses of the commercial representative,

- hand over to the commercial representative a statement about a due commission at the latest on the last day of the month following the semester for which it is due, and
- upon a request of the commercial representative, provide all information, especially the extracts from his accounting book, which has the principal and which needs the commercial representative to verify the amount of the commission belonging to the commercial representative.

The commercial representative is not supposed to be paid by both sides of the deal. Therefore, the claim on the commission and on the agreed reimbursement of the expenses does not arise when the commercial representative, while concluding the concerned business transaction, was active as a commercial representative or intermediary for a person with whom such business transactions is concluded.

For acts done during the commercial representation contract, the commercial representative has a claim on the commission if the business transaction was concluded:

- as a consequence of his activity, or
- with a person whom he got as a customer for business transactions of that kind before the effectiveness of the commercial representation contract.
- For acts done after the termination of the commercial representation contract, the commercial representative has a claim on the commission if the business transaction was concluded:
- chiefly as a consequence of the activity of the commercial representative and in a reasonable time after the termination of the commercial representation contract, or
- based on purchase orders as a consequence of the activities which were just received by the principal or by the commercial representative before the termination of the commercial representation contract.

If the parties have not agreed otherwise, the claim on the commission arises when the principal fulfills or should have fulfilled his obligation from the contract concluded with a third person or when such a third person fulfills or should have fulfilled her obligation. However, if the third person should fulfill her obligation more than six months after the conclusion of the business transaction, the claim on the commission of the commercial representative arises after the conclusion of such a business transaction. As suggested above, the commision is due at the latest on the last day of the month following the trimester when the claim arose.

If, according to the commercial representation contract, the commercial representative has to only arrange for an opportunity for the principal to conclude a certain contract with a third person, the claim of the commercial representative on the commission arises with the procurement of such an opportunity.

The contractual parties may agree upon a non-competition clause prohibiting the commercial representative for a period not execeeding two years after the expiration of the commercial representation contract, in the determined territory or regarding a determined circle of people within such a territory, to conduct on his account or somebody else's account an activity which was a subject matter of the commercial representation contract or other activity competing with the enrepreneurship of the principal. The court has a moderation right and can restrict such a non competion clause or even proclaim it as invalid.

The commercial representation contract is concluded for an undetermined period if either the contract states so or the contract lacks any provisions determining the period for which the contract is concluded or the time restriction cannot be implied from the contract. A commercial representation contract concluded for an undetermined period can be terminated by a notice given by either party. The notice period is at least one month for the first year, two months for the second year, three months for the third year and the following years of the validity of commercial representation contract.

A commercial representation contract concluded for a determinated period terminates with its expiration. If contractual parties follow the contract thereafter, the contract transforms into a contract concluded for an undetermined period.

The non breaching party can withdraw from the commercial representation contract including the exclusivity clause.

The commercial representative has a claim on compensation in the case of a termination of the commercial representation contract if:

- he acquired customers for the principal or he significantly developed business transactions with current customers or the principal has significant benefits from business transactions with them, and
- the payment of such a compensation is fair, taking into consideration all circumstances, especially the commission which the commercial representative loses and which is implied from the business transactions done with these customers.

The amount of the compensation cannot exceed the annual commission calculated based on the result from the last five years. If the commercial representation contract lasted a shorter period than five years, then the calculation is done based on the average from the entire contract period. The payment of this compensation does not deprive the commercial representative from his claim on the compensation for damages. However, the commercial representative loses his claim on the compensation for damage if he does not notify the principal, within one year after the termination of the contract, that he is claiming it.

3.2.11 SILENT PARTNERSHIP CONTRACT

By a silent partnership contract, the silent partner commits himself to provide the entrepreneur with a certain investment contribution and so participates in the entrepreneur´s business and the entrepreneur commits himself to pay a part from his net profit after the deduction for the due addition to the back-up fund, if the entrepreneur has to create such a fund, resulting from the share of the silent partner on the business result. The rights and duties vis-à-vis third persons from the business belong only to the entrepreneur.

The silent partnership contract must include an equal determination of the extent of the participation of the silent partner on the profit and loss. The silent partner does not have any duty to increase his contribution in the case of the business loss, i.e. he participates in the loss only up to his investment contribution.

Similar to the rent and sales contract regarding an enterprise, the sales contract on a leased good, the license agreement and the commercial representation contract, the silent partnership contract requires a written form.

The subject matter of the investment contribution of the silent partner is perceived broadly and it can be:

- a certain amount of money,
- a certain item,
- a right, or
- another asset value to be used during entrepreneurship.

The silent partner must hand over the subject matter of his investment contribution to the entrepreneur or to allow him to use it during his entrepreunership in the time designated by the silent partnership contract contract, otherwise without any unnecessary delay after the conclusion of the silent partnership contract.

If the silent partnership contract does not state otherwise, the entrepreneur becomes:

- the owner of the financial amount or movable item,
- the beneficiary regarding the real estate for the life span of the silent partnership contract,
- the beneficiary regarding the exercise of the right for the life span of the silent contract.

The silent partner is allowed to see the business and accounting documentation related to the entrepreneurship in which he participates and is allowed to request a copy of the financial statements.

The financial statements are decisive for the determination of the silent partner share on the entrepreneurship. The claim of the silent partner on his share on the business profit arises within 30 days after the establishment of the financial statements. If the entrepreneur is a legal person, this period starts with the approval of the financial statements according to the Articles of Association, By-laws or Law. The silent partner's share in the loss decreases the silent partner investement contribution. The silent partner's share in the profit increases his investment contribution and the claim on the share in the profit arises when the original investment contribution is attained.

The silent partner participation in the entrepreneurship extinguishes by:

- the expiration of the period for which the silent partnership was concluded,
- the notice if the silent partnership contract was concluded for an undetermined period and the notice should be given, at the latest, six months before the end of the calendar year unless stated otherwise,
- the increase of the silent partner's share in the loss up to the original investment contribution,
- the termination of the entrepreneur business covered by the silent partntership contract,
- the bankruptcy declaration on the assets of the entrepreneur or by the refusal of the insolvency application due to the insufficiency of the entrepreneur's assets,
- the bankruptcy declaration on the assets of the silent partner,
- by a court decision based on a request and for serious reasons.

The silent partner maintains a position of a creditor regarding his orginal investment contribution and, after the termination of the silent partnership contract, he is allowed to request the return of his investment contribution, increased or decreased by the share in the business result.

3.2.12 LETTER OF CREDIT CONTRACT

By the Letter of credit contract, the bank commits to the applicant that, upon a request, it will pay to the beneficiary from the applicant´s account a certain fulfillment if the beneficiary meets certain conditions within a determined time period and the applicant commits to pay to the bank a fee for it. If the fee for the letter of credit agreed upon, the applicant has to pay to the bank a fee usual at the time of the conclusion of the letter of credit contract.

Similar to the rent and sales contract regarding an enterprise, the sales contract on a leased good, the license agreement, the commercial representation contract, and the silent partnership contract, the letter of credit contract requires a written form. According to the letter of credit contract, the bank notifies in a written form and without any unnecessary delay after its conclusion the beneficiary that the bank is opening in his benefit a credit and informs him about the content. The letter of credit must specify:

- the fulfillment to which the bank commits itself (e.g., to pay a certain amount or to accept a promissory note),
- the time of validity of the letter of credit,
- the letter of credit conditions which the beneficiary must meet in the specified time in order to have a claim on fulfillment from the bank – documents (a documentary letter of credit) or other conditions (another letter of credit).

Therefore, in the case of a documentary letter of credit, the bank must provide the beneficiary with the fulfillment if documents described by the letter of credit are duly presented to the bank during the validity of the letter of credit. The bank has a duty to review with a professional care the relation of the presented documents and the compliance of their content with the conditions set by the letter of credit. In the case of another letter of credit, it proceeds in a similar fashion.

The obligation of the bank from the letter of credit is independent upon the relation between the applicant and the beneficiary.

The letter of credit can be:

- either irrevocable, i.e. the bank can, in a written form, change it or modify or cancel it only with the consent of the beneficiary and the applicant, or
- revocable, i.e. the bank can, in a written form, change it, modify it or cancel it in the relation to the beneficiary, until the time when the beneficiary meets conditions set by the letter of credit.

The letter of credit can be confirmed by one bank or by more banks. When the irrevocable letter of credit is confirmed by another bank, the claim of the beneficiary on the fulfillment vis-à-vis the bank arises at the moment when the confirmation of the letter of credit has been notified to the beneficiary. Both banks are responsible vis-à-vis the beneficiary jointly and severally. The bank, which confirms the letter of credit and provides the beneficiary with the fulfillment according to the content of the letter of credit, has a claim on the fulfillment vis-à-vis the bank which has requested the confirmation of the letter of credit.

3.2.13 CHECKING AND SAVING ACCOUNT CONTRACT

By the checking account contract, the bank commits itself to establish an account for the owner from a certain time in a certain currency, to accept financial transfers on it, to pay duly and timely financial amounts out of it or to do to it or out of it other payment transactions, provided the owner of the account has satisfied the requirements of the Law for a checking account contract.

The checking account contract can stipulate that the bank will execute payment orders up to a certain amount even if there are not enough financial funds in the account.

If neither the amount of the fee nor the manner of its determination is agreed upon in the checking account contract, then the owner of the account has to pay a fee usual at the time of the performance.

Similar to the rent and sales contract regarding an enterprise, the sales contract on a leased good, the license agreement, the commercial representation contract, the silent partnership contract, and the letter of credit contract, the checking account contract requires a written form.

In the checking account contract, the bank designates the owner of the account, which is a legal person, by the indication of:

- his commercial denomination,
- his seat, and
- his identification number.

In the checking account contract, the bank designates the owner of the account, which is a natrual person, by the indication of:

- his first name and last name or his commercial denomination,
- his domicile or his place of business and
- his birth numer or his date of birth or his identification number.

The checking account contract can mention as well:

- any persons allowed to dispose with the finances on the checking account and the manner of the allowed disposition,
- the amount or the manner of determination of the amount of the interest rate and the due time regarding interests or the provision that the interests are not to be paid,

- periods during which the bank notifies the owner of the account about accepted deposits and payments and about executed payouts and payments and the balance of the checking account and the form of these notifications,
- the amount or the manner of the determination of the amount of the fee and the manner how the fee will be paid by the account owner or a provision that the fee will be not requested by the bank. The fee can be agreed upon by a reference to the price list of the bank.

If the checking account is open for more persons, then each of them is in the position of the checking account owner. The co-owners dispose with the checking account jointly, unless the checking account contract provides that only one of them disposes with the account. If neither the checking account contract nor the decision of the court states otherwise, the shares of the co-owners regarding the finances on the checking account are equal.

Another person than the owner of the checking account can dispose with the checking account only based upon a special power of attorney given to that person by the owner of the checking account and the signature of the owner of the checking account on the power of attorney needs to be verified by the bank or by a notary public.

Only persons included on the signature sample, given by the owner of the checking account to the bank, and persons according to the checking account contract are allowed to dispose with the financial funds in the checking account. The signature sample must meet the requirements for a power of attorney. The bank is allowed to dispose with the financial funds in the checking account if the Law or the checking account contract provides so.

Unless the checking account contract provides otherwise, the bank has to inform, through the extract from the checking account, the owner of the checking account monthly about the deposits and payments and annually about the balance.

Unless the checking account contract provides otherwise, the bank pays interest from the balance of the financial funds to the owner of the checking account. The interest rate is fixed as annual and if it is not provided otherwise, it is a half of the discount rate set by the Czech National Bank on the day when the interest should be written to the balance of the financial funds on the checking account.

In default of any provisions in the checking account contract, the interest is on the end of every calendar month and the Bank has to write it to the balance of the financial funds on the checking account in five days after the end of the calendar month for what they are due at the latest.

Neither the checking account contract nor the power of attorney for the disposition with the financial fund is terminated by the death of the owner of the checking account. The bank continues to conduct the payment transactions based on the orders given by the checking account owner or by the empowered person. If it is clearly and honestly proven to the bank that a trustee of the deceased estate has been named and that he is allowed to manage the checking account of the deceaed checking account owner, then such a trustor has rights and duties as the owner of the checking account and the bank follows his instructions.

The checking account contract can be terminated by the owner at any time by a written notice, even if the contact has been concluded for a determined period. The checking account contract terminates on the day of the receipt of the notice by the bank.

The checking account contract can be terminated by the bank at any time by a written notice. The checking account contract terminates on the last day of the calendar month following the month when the notice has been delivered to the checking account owner. However, in the case of a fundamental breach of the checking account contract, the termination occurs already with the receipt of the notice by the checking account owner. If the checking account owner declines to receive the notice or if it is impossible to deliver the notice to the checking account owner, the effects of the receipt occurs on the day when the mail carrier returned the notice to the bank.

In the case of the termination of the checking account contract, the bank settles, without any unnecessary delay and in accordance with the Law on payment relations, all receivables and obligations related to the checking account, cards, forms of cheques, which bank has issued to it. After the settlement of receivables and obligations related to the checking account, the bank pays off the remaining balance of the financial funds to the checking account owner, closes the checking account and notifies the owner of the checking account about the day of closing of the checking account.

By the deposit account contract, the bank commits to establish an account from a certain time and in a certain currency for its owner and to pay based on the financial funds on the account interests and the owner of the account commits to deposit financial funds on the account and allow the bank to use them for a determined or undetermined period with an in advance designated notice period. If the owner of the account disposes with the financial funds in the account before the designated time or before the expiration of the designated notice period, the claim on the interests from the financial funds either expires or is reduced.

Similarly to the rent and sales contract regarding an enterprise, the sales contract on a leased good, the licence agreement, the commercial representation contract, the silent partnership contract, the letter of credit contract, and the checking account contract, the deposit account contract requires a written form.

The deposit account contract can mention as well:

- persons allowed to dispose with the finances on the deposit account,
- the amount or the manner of determination of the amount of the interests, which the bank pays based on the balance of the account to the owner of the deposit account,
- periods during which the bank notifies the owner of the account about accepted deposits and payments and about executed payouts and payments and the balance of the deposit account and the form of these notifications,

- agreement whether, and under which conditions, the owner of the account can dispose with the financial funds on the account before the period designated by the deposit account contract or before the expiration of the notice period.

The bank has to pay to the owner of the account interests agreed upon in the deposit account contract. If neither the interest rate nor the manner of its determination is agreed upon in the deposit account contract, the interest rate is a half of the Lombard interest set by the Czech National Bank for the day on which the interest is written to the financial funds on the account. The interest is due at the latest on the end of each calendar year, except in the case when the financial funds are deposited for a shorter period.

Regarding other issues, the deposit account contract follows the legal regime of the checking account contract.

3.3 SPECIAL REGULATION ON CONTRACTUAL RELATIONS IN INTERNATIONAL COMMERCE

The intensive development of international commerce and the progressing globalization implies a need to regulate international commercial obligations.

The Commercial Code includes such a special regulation and therefore the below mentioned regime (see chapter 3.3.1. general provisions and chapter 3.3.2. special provisions) applies along with the above mentioned regulation of commercial obligations (see chapter 3.1. the general regulation of commercial obligations and chapter 3.2. the special regulation of selected commercial obligations) to relations which are governed by the Czech Law and which at the same time includes one party having it's seat, place of business, or domicile address in the territory of another state than the remaining parties. The rules of International Private Law sets out whether the relations are governed by the Czech Law, possibly by the Commercial Code. Since the International Private Law is dominated by the principle of parties' autonomy, the contractual parties can influence and, even by their agreement, select or reject the application of the legal regime of one of them.

3.3.1 GENERAL PROVISIONS ON CONTRACTUAL RELATIONS IN INTERNATIONAL COMMERCE

The commercial customs generally respected in international commerce in the relevant business field are considered while determining the rights and duties from international commercial obligations, provided they breach neither the contract nor the Law. If the contract expressly refers to these commercial customs, then they take priority over non mandatory provisions of the Commercial Code.

The sources of regulation of international commercial relations with the validity for the Czech Republic can be hierarchically classified as follows:

- international treaties published and binding for the Czech Republic;
- mandatory provisions, namely mandatory provisions of the Commercial Code;
- customs mentioned by the contract;
- non mandatory provisions of the Commercial Code;
- customs not mentioned by the contract.

Naturally, the E.U. Law and the Constitutional Law of the Czech Republic belong to the top positions of this hierarchy of sources of legal regulation.

Each party has to arrange for official permissions on it's side:

- the debtor has to duly apply for an export permission, a transit permission or other official permissions needed for the fulfillment of the obligation in the designated place of the fulfillment and

- the creditor has to duly apply for an import permission or other permissions needed for the fulfillment of the obligation in the designated place of the fulfillment.

If the application of the applicant is finally rejected, the fulfillment is considered to become impossible with all legal consequences. The inability for the obtaining of an official permission is not considered to be a circumstance excluding the responsibility. The party applying in vain for a permission has to compensate the other party for a damage caused by the extinction of the obligation, unless the contract has been concluded with a condition precedent regarding the obtaining of the permission. The provisions of the Civil Code connecting the obtaining of a necessary official decision with the effectivity of the contract and implying from the failure to obtain such a decision within three years after the conclusion of the contract the withdrawal from the contract do not apply to the international commercial obligations

The debtor must fulfill his financial obligation in the agreed currency. In the absence of a different regulation, if the debtor is bound to compensate for the damage caused by the breach of the contract or by the termination of the contract, he pays it in the same currency. In addition, in the case of the default with the payment, the interests in the same currency are due. The middle exchange rate between both currencies at the time of the financial fulfillment in the place designated by the contract is decisive for the currency exchange recalculation. If the place is not designated by the contract, then the seat, place of business or domicile address of the creditor are considered instead.

3.3.2 SPECIAL PROVISIONS ON CONTRACTUAL RELATIONS IN INTERNATIONAL COMMERCE

The Commerce Code mentions expressly regarding contractual relations in international trade the possibility to agree upon the following five clauses:

- on the prohibition of the re-export;
- on the sales restriction;

- on the currency;
- on the sales exclusivity;
- on the tied together trade.

The contractual parties can include in a written sales contract a clause prohibiting a further export. According to such a clause, the buyer is liable to the seller that no one will re-export the purchased merchandise into the designated area. If the re-export occurs in whatsoever manner, the buyer has to compensate the seller´s damage. Further, the buyer must extend a co-operation and must among.else prove upon a seller´s request where the merchandise is located or whether it was consumated without any re-export. If it is unclear from which territory is the re-export prohibited, it is assumed that it is the state territory where the merchandise should have been sent by the seller according to the sales contract. If this determination does not work, then it is the state where the buyer had his seat, place of business or domicile address at the time of the delivery of the merchandise. The reasons for an agreement upon the prohibition of a re-export can be based on international treaties or on the Law of the exporter or on the need to protect the intellectual property. In this context, it is necessary to keep in mind the regulation of business competition on the national level as well as on the E.U. level and their prohibition (possibly declaration as invalid) of all agreements not compatible or negatively influencing the common market. When contractual parties breach this and conclude an agreement not in compliance with the national or European law, such an agreement is invalid and the parties may be sanctioned.

Another possible written clause in contracts in the international trade is the restriction of the sale, which restricts or prohibits the seller regarding the sale of a certain merchandise to a certain circle of customers. As with the prohibition of the re-export, the sales restriction must not breach the national as well as the European regulation of the business competition.

The validity of the sales restriction clause is conditioned by the validity of the related sales contract. In addition, if the purpose of the sales restriction is not the fulfillment of duties stipulated by an international contract or by the protection of the industrial property, the sales restriction clause loses its´ force with the breach of the contract by the buyer or after the expiration of two years from the delivery of the merchandise.

The currency clause is relatively common in international trade. It is a contractual provision setting a certain exchange rate for the currency in which the obligation is fulfilled (the secured currency). If, after the conclusion of the contract, it occurs the change of the exchange rate between the currencies, the debtor has to pay the amount in the secured currency increased or decreased in the manner that the amount in the securing currency remains the same. The currency clause does not require a written form. If decisive currency rates are not set, it is assumed that the method used should be the middle exchange valid in the state where the debtor has it's seat, place of business or domicile address at the time of the conclusion of the contract and at the time when the financial obligation is due.

The sales exclusivity clause prohibits the provider from directly or indirectly providing other people than the purchaser or clients designated by the contract with the merchandise designated in the contract during the time of the validity of the contract. Similar to the prohibition of re-export and sales restriction, the sales exclusivity must be agreed upon in a written form. It is another clause with potential consequences for the business competition and is even sometimes considered to be a special case of the sales restriction provision. It neither prohibits the provider to conduct any advertising and a market research in the designated area nor substitutes individual sales contracts. Therefore, an exclusive sales contract is to some extent a framework agreement as a base for individual sales contracts. In the absence of any different provisions, an exclusive sales contract is valid for one year. A breach of an exclusive sales contract, regardless of whether by the provider or by the purchaser, can establish a claim on withdrawal.

The tied trade contracts represent special and not typical business deals when the form of a direct sales contract does not satisfy the parties. The connection of the export and import, the intra-linking of contracts as well as payments in various currencies (e.g., reciprocial deals, barters) are characteristic for these business deals. They are often a result of international payment difficulties and devision restrictions.

Nowadays, their volume and importance are declining. The Commercial Code treats them as:

- dependent contracts (a principal contract and a secondary contract) and
- multilateral bartered deals.

If it results from the contract, or from circumstances during which the parties concluded the contract, and which were known to both parties at the time of the conclusion of the contract, that the fulfillment from one contract (the principal contract) depends upon the fulfillment from another contract (the secondary contract), the fulfillment of the secondary contract is assumed to be a suspensive condition for the force of the principal contract and if the fulfillment of the principal contract is or should be in advance, then the non fulfillment of the secondary contract operates as a condition of cancellation. Contrariwise, the multilateral bartered trades are trades between parties from different states where the sales price should be settled only between parties having their seat, place of business or domicile address on the territory of the same state. The relations arising from the multilateral bartered trades are governed by the valid regulation on sales contracts. Nevertheless, none of the parties in a multilateral bartered trade can postpone the delivery of the merchandise to another party in a different state only because another party from such a state failed to satisfy him. Parties in a multilateral bartered trade from one state guarantee jointly and severally for the fulfillment of the obligation of each of them in respect to parties from other states. After the fulfillment of an obligation by one party of the multilateral bartered trade, another party can withdraw from the contract only if it provides a compensation for damages caused by the withdrawal.

4. Competition Law

4.1 Protection of Competition

Under the rule of Act No. 173/1991 Collection of Law of the Czech National Council on 26th April 1991, the Czech Office for the Protection of Economic Competition was established, which started its operation on 1st July 1991. Brno was selected as its official residence. It became the central body of public services of the Czech Republic with authorities in the field of protection of economic competition, control of assigning public contracts, and monitoring and coordinating public support. The legal regulations of economic competition have a long-term tradition in the territory of the Czech Republic, which we will try to survey.

The first known legal regulation comes from year 1870, which was incorporated into the legal Act No. 43/1870 ř.z. (country administration), by which §§ 479, 480, and 481 of the general penal law from year 1852 were repealed. At that time the law banned the employers' conventions of decreasing wages or making bad working conditions. At the same time the workers' agreements of work stoppage in order to gain higher wages or creating better working conditions were being banned. Thus under sanctions of contract invalidity, both common agreements of employers and employees were banned. Hereat the law threatened both with sanctions of invalidity of these contracts, but it also threatened the persons, who would intend to realize such contracts, with prison sentence of the period from eight days up to three months. This law was not repealed until year 1950 by the Penal Law No. 86 Collection. Nevertheless, the real beginnings of the protection of economic competition refer to the time of the First Czechoslovak Republic. In year 1927 the first law of unfair competition (Act No. 111/1927 Collection of Law) came into operation, whose aim was to ensure good manners of economic competition. As breaching the rules of competition was considered for example unfair advertising, incorrect designation of origin of goods, misapplication of company trademarks, infringement, and abuse of business and production secrets, and corruption. Protection was present both at the private legal level and the penal one. The private legal protection consisted in the possibility of instituting legal proceedings against holding up unfair action and removing the status, eventually also filing an action for damages. At the level of criminal law every competitor could file a private penal action, as well as every corporation, which according to its code of rules was summoned to defend the competitors' economic interests. The infringers of this law were threatened with a sentence of imprisonment of up to six months. This law was repealed by the new Civil Code in year 1950.

Besides the stated legal regulation, as a matter of course, the state regulated the economic sphere via indirect forms such as taxes, customs duties, budget, and similar tools. A radical change in this regard was brought by the economic recession in the thirties, which motivated the acceptance of an extensive body of systematic regulative measures from the state side. Compulsory syndicalization became widely utilized. It was exerted namely in the field of glass production (Statutory Order No. 2/1936 Collection of Law), textile manufacture (Statutory Order No. 228/1936 Collection of Law), but also timber harvesting (Statutory Order No. 170/1933 Collection of Law, as amended by legal Acts) and other industries.

A compulsory syndicate was established if a number of entrepreneurs in a particular area, the so-called authoritative part (e.g. in the field of glass industry this contained entrepreneurs to whom accrued at least 70 % of the total amount of wages and salaries or revenues for merchandise or number of employees), set by a legal regulation, requested its establishment. The authorities of a compulsory syndicate, where all producers of a particular business were forced to enter, covered for example defining the highest permitted volume of production and sales, setting conditions for transfer of production and sale possibilities among the members, care of import and export and so on. The syndicate was entitled to form its local branches and supervisory bodies. Its activities were controlled by a conservator.

Another way of regulation was a quota system of production. In this case no special organisation forms were established, but legal enactments defined what amounts of products could be manufactured in the particular industries. For example the legal Act No. 105/1932 Collection of Law set a maximal amount of sugar production; the Statutory Order No. 51/1934 Collection of Law authorized the Department of Industry to assign a quota to particular producers of edible fat from the totally set annual volume.

The legal Act No. 141/1933 Collection of Law modified establishing and operating of cartels and private monopolies. The concept of cartel was delimited as an agreement among independent entrepreneurs who undertook themselves to limit or except freedom of competition, respectively by arranging production, sales, business conditions, and so on if the purpose of contract was to corner the market most efficiently. The law acknowledged the present cartels and at the same time repealed the provisions of the Coalition Act which banned cartels.

Cartels could be founded partly according to the regulations of the Commercial Code on the basis of simple contracts or as institutions of a permanent character. In the interest of ensuring control, the cartel contracts had to be in a written form and had to be recorded in the Register of the State Statistical Office. Moreover, cartel prices and rates were registered as well as interferences with entities standing beyond the cartel. Provided that public interest could be threatened by operation of a cartel agreement, reconciliation was introduced. Moreover, the government was authorized to inhibit operation of the cartel agreement in case an entrepreneurial activity in a particular industry was threatened by high prices. Cartel commissions and cartel court were also appointed, which supervised whether stipulated duties were not neglected.

The quoted law incorporated also the regulation regarding a withdrawal from a contract, which could happen in case that by its provision entrepreneurial activities were considerably economically threatened, aggravated or precluded at such a level which could not be anticipated at concluding the contract even if the concerned entity respected the duties of a respectable businessman.

With the exception of the defined parts (e.g. incorporation, duty to report prices) a similar regime was applied also at private monopolies.

In order to realize the cartel law, several procedural regulations were issued, namely those regarding maintenance of the cartel register and collection of deeds, reconciliation, procedure at solving excessive prices, etc.

In point of state intervention, the legal Act No. 95/1933 Collection of Law of extraordinary mandatory power (as amended by legal Acts) became quite substantial. This Act authorized the government, at the times of extraordinary economic circumstances, to regulate the customs tariff via its provisions and to take measures for an adequate adjustment of prices, production and sales conditions in the industry, trade and agriculture, as well as maintaining balance in the state economy, state companies or companies managed by state, institutes, funds and other establishments and institutions to which the law would be otherwise required. Its regulations had to be submitted to the Parliament within the period of 14 days and in case both the Chambers refused to consent, it became ineffective. Based on the so-called Enabling Act a succession of statutory orders regarding various sides of economy was issued in the subsequent years.

In the post-war period the cartel law was still valid for a certain time; nevertheless, in consideration of the current situation it was not utilized in practice. It was de facto annulled by the Constitution in year 1948 (The Constitution issued on 9th May).

In the socialistic period the competition law in fact disappeared from our legal order. Indeed the planned economic abuse of the dominating position of economic units excluded it. Specific adjustments of unfair competitive behaviour were provided in relation to the reformative endeavours in years 1968 – 1969. Namely the Statutory Order No. 169/1969 Collection of Law, which amended the Statutory Order No. 100/1966 Collection of Law, brought a detailed adjustment of behaviour of socialistic organisations, which was not allowed to be in discordance with good manners of competition and prohibited to harm other competing organisations. According to this rule, an organisation which was harmed or threatened by behaviour, which was in discordance with good manners of competition, was entitled to claim the other organisation to refrain from such behaviour, to eliminate the unlawful situation and to indemnify for losses, including the lost profit. The Statutory Order prohibited the organisations to misuse their market position in order to gain unjustified or inadequate advantages at the expense of other organisations.

As an abuse of market position was considered namely the following:

a) enforcing inadequate economic conditions at entering into a contract of supplying or providing services (namely a contract of performance which is at the time of concluding a contract in an obvious disproportion towards performance of the provided organisation or an agreement of unjustified lower possession consequence in case of breaching contractual obligations beyond those supportably established by a legal regulation),

b) binding of entering into a contract of supplying or providing services for the subsequent supplementary performance, which is not, according to economic practice, connected with the subject matter of the contract.

The Statutory Order clearly stipulated that socialistic organisations were not allowed to misuse the market situation in a way which could provoke disorder on the market, namely to stop or reduce production or sale of goods, conceal or accumulate goods in order to incite its lack for the purposes of maintaining or unjustified increasing of prices or gaining other unauthorised economic profit. Organisations, neither on their own nor in agreement with other organisations, were allowed to permit such behaviour which could lead to exclusion or elimination of competition, which would, in discordance with the interests of development of the national economy, unfavourably influence the market conditions at the expense of other organisations or at the consumers' expense.

Nevertheless, the Statutory Order from year 1969 was annulled by the Statutory Order No. 14/1971 Collection of Law, and the only regulation which was taken over into the amended Economic Code in year 1970 was the one which forbade organisations to abuse their economic monopoly position towards other organisations and which was, in accordance with the former conception of negation of market and competition, classified under the head of "cooperation of socialistic organisations". However, this regulation remained unutilised in practice.

The return towards the law of competition thus accrued at the beginning of nineties by accepting the Law of Economic Competition in year 1991 (No. 63/1991 Collection of Law), which was amended in years 1992 and 1993. The amendments were enforced namely by the necessity of harmonisation of the Czech law with the law of the European Community, i.e. adjustment of the Czech Law of Competition in the articles 85 and 86 of the Contract of the European Economic Community.

Thereafter the law from year 1991 was substituted by the present legal regulation incorporated into the Law of the Protection of Economic Competition No. 143/2001 Collection of Law, which came into force on 1st July 2001, which was adopted for the purpose of a full compatibility with the law of the European Union, sc. in all the areas of the Public Competition Law.

In order to protect economic competition, the Czech Office for the Protection of Economic Competition was established fifteen years ago by the legal Act No. 173/1991 Collection of Law of the Czech National Council from 26th April 1991, which commenced its operation on 1st July 1991. In year 1992 the Office was substituted by the Ministry for Economic Competition. However, on 1st November 1996 the above-mentioned ministry changed into the present Office for the Protection of Economic Competition. The competence of the Office is delimitated by the legal Act No. 273/1996 Collection of Law, as amended by the Act No. 187/1999 Collection of Law. The Office is one of the central bodies of public administration headed by a chairman appointed based on the proposal of the President of the Czech Republic. It has gained respect due to its activities for the years of its operation and has become an essential part of the state mechanism in the Czech Republic.

4.2 UNFAIR COMPETITION

Unfair competition as such is provided for by the Commercial law and it is expressly prohibited by its provisions. According to this code, unfair competition is defined as actions taken in terms of economic competition which are contrary to good manners of competition and which are capable of causing loss, harm or damage to other competitors or consumers.

Unfair competition especially refers to:

a) *Deceptive advertising* which is defined as spreading or disclosing data or information regarding one's own or other people's business, its products or services which are capable to create a deceptive image or misapprehension and thus gaining advantage for oneself, one's business or other people's business in terms of economic competition at the expense or to the detriment of other competitors or consumers. Spreading or disclosing information according to the Commercial Code is defined as any communication whether verbal or written, printed, graphical, photographic, broadcast via radio, television or by any other communication media. Even a truthful statement or disclosure can be considered deceptive in case that such can be misleading with respect to the circumstances and connections under which it was made.

b) *False designation of origin of goods and services*, is any designation which, in commercial intercourse, may create a misconception that the goods or services thus designated come from a certain state, area or place, or are made by a certain producer or that they have certain characteristic features or special qualities. It is irrelevant whether such designation was stated directly on the goods, packaging or business documents etc. It is equally irrelevant whether false designation was made directly or indirectly and by what means it was made. False designation is also understood as incorrect designation of goods or services to which an addition is attached serving to distinguish it from its real origin, using terms such as "kind", "type", "manner" and if such designation is still capable of creating a misconception regarding the origin or character of the goods or services. However, a designation is not considered as deceptive if a name is used which has become established as a usual term for the designation of type and quality of goods or services in commercial intercourse unless additions attached thereto are capable of misleading in terms of origin such as "genuine", "original" etc.

c) *Creating the danger of confusion*, which is:

– the use of a company name or name of a person or of a special company designation already rightfully used by another competitor,

– the use of special company designations or special designations or designs of products, services or business materials of a company which are commonly known among the customers to be used as specific for a certain company or factory (such as designation of packaging, printed matter, printed forms, catalogues, promotional items),

– imitation of somebody else's products, their packaging or services, unless these are imitated in features which by their nature are functionally, technologically or aesthetically so predetermined and the imitator has taken all possible measures which can be reasonably expected from him to eliminate or at least substantially limit the danger of confusion, if such actions are capable of creating the danger of confusion or misconception regarding association with a particular company, firm, special designation or products or services of another competitor.

d) *Benefiting from the reputation of another company, products or services of another competitor*, is the use of the reputation of a business, products or services of another competitor for the purpose of gaining benefit for oneself or another person's business which would otherwise not be achieved by a competitor.

e) *Bribery* are actions by which:

f) a competitor directly or indirectly offers, promises or provides any benefit to a person who is a member of a statutory body or another body of another competitor or who is in employment or similar relationship with another competitor, in order to achieve illegitimate advantage or benefit in competition for oneself or another competitor by dishonest actions of such person at the expense of other competitors,

g) or if such person directly or indirectly demands, solicits or accepts any benefit for the above purpose.

h) *Defamation* are actions by which a competitor states or spreads untruthful information about the status, products or services of another competitor which may result in harm to such competitor in any way. Defamation is also understood as stating and/or spreading truthful information about the status, products or services of another competitor if such actions may result in harm to that competitor. Such actions, however, are not considered unfair competition if a competitor was forced to take such actions (justifiable defence)

i) *Comparative advertising* is any type of advertising which explicitly or indirectly identifies another competitor or the goods or services by another competitor.

j) Comparative advertising is only admissible if:

    −   it is not deceptive and/or does not use deceptive commercial practices according to special legal regulations,

    −   it only compares goods or services designed to satisfy the same needs or predetermined for the same purpose,

- it objectively compares one or more basic features or characteristics of given goods or services which are significant, verifiable and characteristic for them, this can also include the price,

- it does not create the danger of confusion of the entity whose products or services are promoted by the advertisement with a competitor or among their companies, goods or services, trademarks, firms or other special designations which have become characteristic for one of them in the market,

- it does not disparage, by untruthful information, the business, goods or services of a competitor nor his trademarks, firm or other special designations which have become characteristic for the competitor, nor his activities, status or other circumstances regarding the competitor,

- it refers to products for which the competitor is entitled to use trademark-protected designation of origin, always solely for those products with the same designation of origin,

- it does not result in unfair benefit from the reputation and good will connected with the competitor's trademark, his firm or other special designations which have become characteristic for the competitor, or from the good will connected with the designation of origin of the rival goods, and

- it does not offer goods or services as imitations or reproductions of goods or services designated by a trademark or trade name or firm.

Any comparison referring to a special offer must be clearly and unambiguously specified by a date by which such offer expires or it must state that such offer will be subject to availability of the goods or services offered. If a special offer has not taken effect yet, the competitor also has to state a date of commencement of the period during which special offer price is applicable or any other special conditions.

k) *Divulging trade secrets* are actions through which a person without authorization discloses or makes available or uses for his own or other person's benefit the trade secrets which may be used in terms of competition and which was disclosed to him:

- by entrusting him with secret information or otherwise making it available to him (such as through technical blueprints, manuals, drawings, models, designs) in relation to his employment or professional relationship to the competitor or in relation to other relationships to him or, as the case may be, when discharging the duties entrusted to him by a court of law or by another body,

- through his own or other person's actions contrary to the law.

l) Threatening the consumers' health and the environment are actions through which a competitor distorts the conditions of economic competition by producing or marketing products or providing services posing threat to the interests of protection of health or the environment protected by the law in order to gain benefit for himself or for another person at the expense of other competitors or consumers.

Persons whose rights have been infringed or affected by unfair competition may demand from the infringer that he refrains from such unfair conduct and that he rectifies the infringement. Further these persons may demand reasonable compensation which can also be rendered to them in pecuniary form, compensation for damages and surrendering of the wrongfully obtained benefit.

LITERATURE

BARTOŠÍKOVÁ, M. – ŠTENGLOVÁ, I.: Společnost s ručením omezeným. Praha : C.H.Beck 2006

ČERNÁ, S.: Obchodní právo. Akciová společnost. Praha : ASPI 2006

DĚDIČ, J. – ČECH, P.: Evropská akciová společnost. Praha : Polygon 2006

DĚDIČ, J. A KOL.: Obchodní zákoník. Komentář. Praha : Polygon 2002

DĚDIČ, J. – KŘÍŽ, R. – ŠTENGLOVÁ, I.: Akciová společnost. Praha : C.H.Beck 2007

DVOŘÁK, T.: Komanditní společnost. Praha : ASPI 2004

DVOŘÁK, T.: Společnost s ručením omezeným. Praha : ASPI 2008

DVOŘÁK, T.: Akciová společnost a Evropská akciová společnost. Praha : ASPI 2005

DVOŘÁK, T.: Družstevní právo. Praha : C.H.Beck 2006

ELIÁŠ, K.: Kurz obchodního práva. Úvodní a obecná část. Soutěžní právo. 5. vydání, C. H. Beck :

Praha 2007

ELIÁŠ, K. - BARTOŠÍKOVÁ, M. - POKORNÁ, J.: Kurz obchodního práva. Právnické osoby jako podnikatelé. 5. vydání, C.H.Beck : Praha 2006

Lochmanová, L.: Základy obchodního práva. Ostrava, KEY Publishing 2009

Pelikánová, I.: Obchodní právo, 1 – 2 díl. Praha : ASPI 2005 – 2006

Pelikánová, I.: Komentář k obchodnímu zákoníku. 1 – 2 díl. Praha : ASPI 2004

Štenglová, I. a kol.: Obchodní zákoník. Komentář. Praha 2009